MW00758192

TRAGEDY

APRIL 27, 2011   *TO*   JANUARY 9, 2012

TRIUMPH

HOW THE ALABAMA FOOTBALL TEAM HELPED LIFT A COMMUNITY

www.kcisports.com

The Birmingham News

PRESS-REGISTER

The Huntsville Times

Graphic design by Elizabeth Chick
Cover design by Adrian Gonzalez
Cover photo by Hal Yeager
Printed in the United States of America

ISBN 978-0-9843882-3-3 (soft cover)

ISBN 978-0-9837337-4-4 (hard cover)

This book is available in quantity at special discounts for your group or
organization. For further information, contact:
KCI Sports Publishing
3340 Whiting Avenue Suite 5
Stevens Point, WI 54481
1-800-697-375

www.kcisports.com

Ringheads gather in Champions Square before the BCS
championship game.

PHOTO/MICHAEL DEMOCKER

PREFACE

On April 27, 2011, no one was thinking about football.

Even Bryant-Denny stadium could stand merely as a backdrop to the behemoth tornado that ripped through Tuscaloosa. As storms rampaged across Alabama, we sought physical shelter wherever possible, but found strength and comfort in our families, our friends and our faith.

There was so much pain in those first days after the storms. A tragedy so widespread can be difficult to comprehend. But with each day, Alabama's residents banded closer together and worked relentlessly to begin the recovery process.

Many of us have settled into a new "normal," a post-storm routine that includes so many of the things about which we've spent our lives being passionate.

And in Alabama, that means football.

As we cheer Alabama's second national championship in three years, we celebrate knowing recent challenges make it just a little bit sweeter. The opportunity to right this season's earlier loss to LSU in the BCS "Rematch of the Century" certainly wasn't the preferred path, but Alabama got the job done in spectacular fashion.

The defense was ferocious while the offense was steady, and Alabama rolled over LSU 21-0 in the first shutout in BCS Championship game history. As coach Nick Saban said after the game, it truly was a team victory.

Congratulations to Alabama and all its fans on this historic win. We hope you enjoy this commemorative book that chronicles the season and Alabama's "Road to Recovery" since the storms.

Amazingly, this marks the third consecutive commemorative book *The Birmingham News*, *Press-Register* of Mobile and *The Huntsville Times* have published after a BCS Championship (Alabama 2010, Auburn 2011, Alabama 2012).

That is a remarkable run by a truly remarkable state.

Roll Tide!

Ricky Mathews
Pam Siddall
Kevin Wendt

Ricky Mathews
President of Alabama Advance Newspapers
Publisher, Press Register

Pam Siddall
President, Birmingham News Multimedia

Kevin Wendt
Editor, The Huntsville Times

FOREWORD

As dawn approached on the morning of April 30th, I was in the Rosedale community meeting with our first responders. When the sun rose over the horizon, it began to illuminate the devastation that had engulfed our city. In this moment, for the first time, the totality of what had transpired became all too real.

Over the previous 60 hours, I had seen thriving neighborhoods removed from the map and talked to hundreds of people, who were among the thousands then homeless. I had met with business owners who had lost everything and countless individuals who became unemployed in a matter of minutes. I had stood in deserted intersections where tens of thousands of cars once traveled and seen our neighborhoods now being protected by the National Guard. I had met with family members who had lost loved ones or who were still searching the debris fields for a sign of life.

My story is one among many, and in the months following April 27th, our citizens have been writing new chapters that have demonstrated to the world our confident hope. That is what makes the University of Alabama's win over LSU on January 9th so meaningful.

The Crimson Tide's journey to the BCS National Championship has mirrored our residents' journey toward recovery. Since April 27, 2011, we all have experienced successes in the face of withering adversity. Words such as resiliency, dedication and comeback, which were mostly used to describe the gridiron, now apply to our residents as they too fight back to reclaim their future.

To say the least, there is something special about this championship season which was preceded by tragedy. We've been inspired by football players and coaches who volunteered throughout the city and witnessed firsthand the fierce resolve of long-snapper Carson Tinker as he faced unimaginable grief with resolve, dignity and grace. In our hearts, it is safe to say that Alabama's dedication to our residents off the field far outweighed their superiority on the field.

Forged in tragedy, this 14th National Championship is a story of hope that will continue to inspire us to rebuild our communities in a way that honors all those who have been through so much.

Sincerely,

Walter Maddox
Mayor of Tuscaloosa

Mayor Walter Maddox meets with President Obama after the April 27 tornado.

Alabama's Dre Kirkpatrick celebrates after the BCS National Championship college football game. AP PHOTO/DAVE MARTIN

TABLE OF CONTENTS

BCS Championship Game 8

April 27, 2011 Tornado 34

Pre Season 46

Alabama vs. Kent State 48

Coaches 54

Alabama vs. Penn. State 56

Alabama Defense 62

Alabama vs. North Texas 64

Alabama vs. Arkansas 68

Alabama vs. Florida 74

Alabama vs. Vanderbilt 80

Jesse Williams 84

Alabama vs. Ole Miss 86

Alabama vs. Tennessee 92

Courtney Upshaw 98

Alabama vs. LSU 100

Alabama vs. Mississippi State 106

Alabama vs. Georgia Southern 112

Spirit Award 116

Aaron Douglas 117

Alabama vs. Auburn 118

Trent Richardson 124

2011-2012 Final Stats 126

2011-2012 Team Roster 128

ALABAMA CRIMSON TIDE

THE COACHES' TROPHY

THE
NATIONAL
CHAMPION

Alabama running back Trent Richardson tries for extra yardage as LSU defender Lavar Edwards pursues in the first quarter.
PHOTO/MIKE KITTRELL

Alabama quarterback AJ McCarron celebrates as he leaves the field at the half with Alabama leading 9-0. PHOTO/MARK ALMOND

Alabama defender Mark Barron stops LSU wide receiver Rueben Randle as Alabama's Courtney Upshaw closes in during the first quarter. PHOTO/BILL STARLING

TIDE 21 - TIGERS ZEREAUX!

By **IZZY GOULD**

NEW ORLEANS — Revenge was a dish Alabama served up in the Big Easy.

This one was hot and spicy, and meant to leave some Tigers' tongues stinging for many months to come.

On Monday night, for the second time in three seasons, Nick Saban guided Alabama to a BCS national championship with a resounding 21-0 victory over LSU in the Mercedes-Benz Superdome, one that will go down as one of the all-time dominant performances in national championship history.

This time, Saban was the ringmaster in badly whipping the Tigers – a team he led to the 2003 title, the first of three in his career. It was Alabama's 14th national title overall.

There was talk entering the game about the possibility of a split national championship. LSU (13-1) defeated Alabama (12-1) 9-6 in overtime on Nov. 5 in Tuscaloosa, a game settled completely by field goals. But the Crimson Tide was also voted No. 1 in the final Associated Press poll.

Alabama held LSU to 92 total yards, forced two fumbles, an interception by C.J. Mosley and sacked LSU quarterback Jordan Jefferson four times. The unit was led with seven tackles each from linebackers Courtney Upshaw and Jerrell Harris. Upshaw, who was named the game's defensive MVP, had six solo tackles and a sack.

"I got tired of hearing how their team had turnovers and all that," Alabama defensive coordinator Kirby Smart said. "Our guys have pride in that, too. They came out and played tough.

"It means they didn't score, and they have to get better for next year now ... for them to have a shutout ... I certainly didn't think this game was going to be played like this."

Offensively, sophomore quarterback AJ McCarron thrived under offensive coordinator Jim McElwain's game plan, the two working together for the final time before McElwain leaves to begin a new quest as Colorado State's head coach.

McCarron was 23-of-34 passing for 234 yards and was sacked twice.

"Tonight, he was on a whole other level, it actually blew me away," said senior center William Vlachos, an outgoing senior. "... The guy's unbelievable. I don't care what anyone says about him, he wasn't scared at all. I don't know how many million people watched this game on television, it didn't phase him. He came out here and executed against one of the best defenses in college football. You can't say enough about him. He's got a bright future."

As Alabama struggled to find the end zone, placekicker Jeremy Shelley played with plenty of poise, kicking five field goals for the game's first 15 points to give the Tide a two-touchdown lead in the third quarter.

Shelley began the game with a 23-yarder, then collected himself following a blocked 42-yarder in the second quarter to make his next three field goals from 34, 41 and 35 yards.

Shelley set an all-bowl record with seven field goal attempts, and tied an all-bowls record with five made field goals.

"It was a lot of fun," Shelley said. "I had a lot of opportunities."

After seven quarters and one overtime in a combined two games, Alabama finally scored the first touchdown of the season series when Heisman Trophy finalist Trent Richardson broke loose for a 34-yard touchdown run with 4:36 left.

Richardson, who finished the season as Alabama's single-season rushing leader with 1,679 yards and 21 TD runs, played in what is widely believed to be his final game with the Crimson Tide.

Richardson said afterward he will weigh his options in the coming days.

"I'm still trying to figure out how to get in the damn end zone," McElwain said. "... But the last time I checked, we got more than they got, so that's what it meant.

"I'm excited we got a first down. I'm excited we finally got a touchdown. Fitting it was Trent Richardson, who iced it because that guy's a great player."

LSU quarterback Jordan Jefferson is hemmed in by Alabama linebacker Nico Johnson (35) and defensive back DeQuan Menzie (24). PHOTO/MARK ALMOND

Alabama defensive back Dre Kirkpatrick (21) reacts to the crowd during warmups. PHOTO/MARK ALMOND

Alabama defensive lineman Damion Square and linebacker Dont'a Hightower bring down LSU quarterback Jordan Jefferson. PHOTO/MARK ALMOND

GRADING THE TIDE

OFFENSE

A

So what if the Tide scored only one TD? It piled up yards, particularly through the air, ate clock and set up field-goal attempts galore.

DEFENSE

A

A great Alabama defense — maybe the greatest? — saved its best for last. It dominated from start to finish. But a shutout? Inconceivable.

SPECIAL TEAMS

A

Five FGs in seven attempts were redemption for 2-6 on Nov. 5. A 49-yard punt return by Marquis Maze sparked the Tide early.

COACHING

A

Outgoing offensive coordinator Jim McElwain's solid plan — liberal passing — was executed well. Tight ends were used well.

OVERALL

A

This was an Alabama football team on a mission. It thought it was the better team on Nov. 5. Now it has proof and another national championship.

**Assessment by
Don Kausler, Jr.**

Alabama running back Eddie Lacy leaps over LSU safety Brandon Taylor. PHOTO/BILL STARLING

NO DOUBT, NO DISPUTE, NO SPLIT: IT'S ALABAMA

By **KEVIN SCARBINSKY**

NEW ORLEANS – Big-boy football.

That's what Les Miles promised the day before, and that's what his LSU team delivered Monday night in the Superdome.

It was six visits to the scoreboard for Alabama and one trip across midfield for LSU.

It was no points for the Tigers and no doubt about the Crimson Tide.

It was Alabama 21, LSU 0, and now there is no dispute. There is no split and no mayhem after the Allstate BCS National Championship Game.

This was boys against men.

"I think so," Alabama center William Vlachos said. "I think we all brought our big-boy pads tonight. This was a game for men."

It started up front on both sides of the ball with two grizzled veterans from greater Birmingham playing their final college games.

On offense, it was Vlachos, the fifth-year senior center from Mountain Brook, who anchored a line that gave AJ McCarron the kind of protection usually afforded the head coach.

And Nick Saban's guards are armed.

McCarron got Jeremy Shelley close enough to make 5-of-7 field-goal tries and put Trent Richardson in position to thunder 34 yards for the first touchdown of the season between these teams for the final points.

McCarron also proved a point. He joined the fraternity of Alabama national championship quarterbacks by breaking the mold of the most recent members. He was no caretaker, no game manager along for the ride.

He was a playmaker and a leader, hitting 23 of 34 passes for 234 yards with no picks and only two sacks, and he was named the game's offensive MVP. He also became the first sophomore quarterback to pilot a BCS Championship Game victory.

"He was huge," Vlachos said. "I've said it all year. He doesn't get rattled in these situations. Tonight he was on a whole different level. He was a vocal leader. He wasn't scared a bit. He played fantastic.

"I tell you what. The sky's the limit for that guy."

On the other side, Jordan Jefferson and LSU's playmakers spent much of the night staring up at the roof, dragged down early, often and with bad intentions by, as Saban described them with love, a "hateful bunch" of Alabama defenders.

They started a debate early in the season about their place in history and ended it with their greatest statement. LSU ran 44 plays and gained 92 yards. The Tigers crossed midfield once and, for the second time this season against the Tide, the goal line not at all.

That's not domination. That's suffocation. Fifth-year senior nose guard Josh Chapman from Hoover was right in the middle of it, demanding attention so defensive MVP Courtney Upshaw, another senior, could fly to the football.

Who's No. 1 now? There's no question.

"Ain't no doubt," Chapman said. "We knew we were gonna come out and dominate this game. That's what we wanted to do, make it a line-of-scrimmage game. We dominated the line of scrimmage."

This wasn't a complete departure from LSU's 9-6 overtime victory Nov. 5 in Tuscaloosa, the one that sent Alabama into chase-and-hope mode. The Tide had the better numbers in that game, too, and more chances to score.

The result that night didn't shake the Alabama players. It steeled them. They knew something the scoreboard didn't.

"To be honest with you, when we walked off the field the last time we played them, every kid knew," defensive coordinator Kirby Smart said. "Every kid knew who had the better team. We just had to take care of business to have the opportunity to play them again, and we did, and we got lucky to get the opportunity."

True. Stanford, Boise State and Oklahoma State all had to lose to make the rematch possible, but luck had nothing to do with 21-0. With Saban's second BCS championship in the past three years, his third overall. Or with Alabama's 14th national title by the school's count.

Doubt the total if you like, but don't doubt this team. Alabama has the best team in the country.

"I told my team I did not see it coming," Miles said.

The title came and went from boys to men.

BY THE NUMBERS

1   The number of coaches who has won three BCS championship games. Nick Saban got his third on Monday night in Alabama's 21-0 victory over LSU. Saban also won the title with Alabama after the 2009 season and LSU after the 2003 season.

1   Number of teams that has shut out LSU in its past 236 games. Alabama blanked the Tigers for the third time in that span. Monday ended a 121-game LSU scoring streak that started after a 31-0 loss to Alabama in 2002. Alabama also blanked LSU in 1996, 26-0.Ð

7   Times that Alabama has finished No. 1 in the final coaches

poll of the season, which it accomplished again by beating LSU. Alabama also was the No. 1 team in the final coaches polls of 1961, 1964, 1973, 1979, 1992 and 2009.

48   Victories over the past four seasons for Alabama, tying the SEC record for most victories in four years. Florida also won 48 games from 2006 through 2009.

49   Yards on a first-quarter punt return by Alabama WR Marquis Maze against LSU on Monday night — 40 yards more than the Tigers had given up on punt returns all season. Before that punt return, opponents had returned 18 punts for 9 net yards against LSU.

Alabama running back Trent Richardson (3) carries the ball into the end zone in the fourth quarter to score a touchdown.
PHOTO/BILL STARLING

NOTES:

By **DON KAUSLER, JR.**
JON SOLOMON
TOMMY HICKS

SHELLEY SETS KICKING RECORDS

Jeremy Shelley had no idea entering Monday he would try all the field goal attempts in the BCS Championship Game. He ended up tying a bowls record with five field goals and set a bowls record with seven tries.

"I've never tried seven in my life," Shelley said. "Maybe four. It's pretty remarkable to be in this position." Shelley's 15 points scored was the fourth-most by an individual in the BCS Championship Game. That was a long way from Alabama kickers missing four field goals on Nov. 5 in the 9-6 loss to LSU.

"I can't thank my teammates enough for giving me the support to get over the hump and finish the season the way we did," Shelley said. "There was a lot of positive talk, a lot of people telling us they believe in us, and they know maybe it was a bad night."

EXPENSIVE CHAMPIONSHIP GAME TICKETS

StubHub's average sold ticket price a couple hours before kickoff was $1,565, making it the most expensive since the company started tracking these ticket sales five years ago.

The previous high in recent years had been $1,150 for LSU-Ohio State at the Superdome in 2008. Other average prices in recent years: Auburn-Oregon in 2011 ($925) and Alabama-Texas in 2010 ($771).

Twenty-five percent of the buyers at StubHub came from Louisiana and 22 percent came from Alabama. StubHub said the highest listing for an Alabama-LSU ticket was $10,000, and the most expensive purchased was $5,000.

Both were for club-level seats at the 50-yard line. The cheapest ticket purchased was for $973 back in October. Prices on Monday came down to as low as $1,200, which StubHub had not seen since November.

MAZE'S BIG AND HURTFUL RETURN

Marquis Maze's 49-yard punt return in the first half was a shocker against LSU punter Brad Wing. Entering the game, LSU had only allowed six punt return yards all season.

"My whole mindset was to go into this game on special teams to be aggressive," Maze said. "Everyone doubted us the whole time: LSU had a great defense, LSU had a great special teams. And really we showed we're great too." Maze may have gotten even more but pulled up lame with an injured hamstring and left the game. "I could barely walk," Maze said.

SPLIT TITLE? MILES WON'T TOUCH IT

LSU coach Les Miles danced around a question about whether the Tigers deserve a split national title from the Associated Press.

"The only thing I can tell you is we think we had a great year; that this football team had as quality a run as there is in the country," Miles said.

"I think this team accomplished a lot. I think that's for the voters to figure." Alabama became the first team to win the national title without winning a conference title since Minnesota in 1936.

HISTORY FOR THE CRIMSON TIDE

Nick Saban become the only current Football Bowl Subdivision coach with three national championships and the first to win three BCS titles. He jumped ahead of Joe Paterno and Bobby Bowden, the two winningest football coaches in major college history, who each won two national titles.

Alabama joined rare company recently in winning two national titles in a three-year span. Since the late 1980s, only Nebraska, Miami, USC and Florida had accomplished it.

Meanwhile, the state of Alabama won its third straight national championship, the first state to do so in major college football with multiple universities. Since the Associated Press poll started in 1936,

the only other state to do it twice with different teams was Texas, with Texas Christian in 1938 and Texas A&M in 1939.

SOME FANS ARRIVE TO FIND SEATS TAKEN

Dozens of fans arrived at the Superdome for the Allstate BCS Championship Game between No. 1 LSU and No. 2 Alabama to find their seats were taken for auxiliary press seating.

The Associated Press reported the top two rows of the upper deck were turned into an overflow area for the media, with one of the rows covered by tables.

Fans complained that they paid for those seats but wouldn't be allowed to use them. Officials with the Sugar Bowl, who were in charge of hosting the championship this season, quickly found new seats for affected fans closer to the field.

"In making adjustments to accommodate the overwhelming media demand for this game, it was necessary to void seating in the upper (rows) of the stadium," Sugar Bowl spokesman John Sudsbury said. "Apparently, some of that seating was not removed from the saleable manifest." Sudsbury said the bowl had an emergency relocation plan in place that accommodated all involved ticket holders. The mix-up is similar to a situation that occurred at last year's Super Bowl in Arlington, Texas, where some temporary seating had not been inspected and couldn't be used.

STEEN REPLACES MCCULLOUGH AT GUARD

Fifth-year senior Alfred McCullough of Athens started the game at right guard for Alabama, but in the second quarter, he was replaced by Anthony Steen.

Steen started nine games at right guard during the regular season, including the first seven before he suffered a concussion at Ole Miss.

McCullough started two games at right guard and then started two games at left tackle when Barrett Jones was out with an injury. McCullough started at right guard in the regular-season finale at Auburn.

Alabama running back Eddie Lacy makes a gain in the first
quarter against LSU. PHOTO/MIKE KITTRELL

Alabama running back Trent Richardson celebrates as he holds the Coach's Trophy after Alabama defeated LSU.

PHOTO/BILL STARLING

DECISIVE VOTES FOR TIDE ENDS SPLIT-TITLE DEBATE

By **MIKE HERNDON**

NEW ORLEANS — When the New York Giants beat New England in the Super Bowl, they didn't share the NFL championship with the Patriots.

When Muhammad Ali beat Joe Frazier in the Thrilla in Manila, they didn't share the heavyweight title.

When John McEnroe beat Bjorn Borg in the 1980 U.S. Open final, he and Borg didn't raise the trophy together.

All of those victories came in rematches and avenged prior losses, but there was no question who the champ was after the second meeting – or third, in the case of Ali and Frazier.

And now that Alabama has won its rematch with LSU in dominant fashion, there is no doubt that the Crimson Tide is college football's consensus national champion.

As participants in the BCS rankings, the USA Today coaches' poll is required to recognize Monday night's winner as the national champ and did so Monday night, with all 59 voters ranking Alabama No. 1.

The Associated Press poll is under no such restriction, but followed suit Monday night as 54 of the poll's 60 voters picked Alabama No. 1.

Speculation was rampant before Monday night's rematch about whether LSU could lose and still retain a share of the national crown.

Several AP voters said they would consider voting LSU No. 1 even if the Tigers lost.

The Tigers faced one of the toughest schedules of any national contender ever, beating three BCS bowl winners – Oregon, Arkansas and West Virginia – and defeating Alabama 9-6 in overtime in Tuscaloosa in the first meeting between the teams.

At least one was still conflicted even after Alabama's 21-0 victory Monday night.

"What I wish I could do with my final AP ballot: Have a three-way tie for second between Bama, LSU and Oklahoma State. All too flawed for No. 1," tweeted Seth Emerson of the Macon (Ga.) Telegraph and Columbus Ledger-Enquirer.

When the vote came in Monday night, only one voter picked LSU No. 1. Four others cast their No. 1 vote for Oklahoma State, a 41-38 winner over Stanford in the Fiesta Bowl.

It wasn't just that the Crimson Tide won but the way it won that ended the split title debate. Alabama held LSU to only 92 yards and allowed the Tigers to cross midfield only once.

Asked whether his team still deserved consideration for a No. 1 vote, LSU coach Les Miles was noncommittal.

Alabama fans scream as the Crimson Tide takes the field for warm-ups before the start of the BCS Championship game. PHOTO/BILL STARLING

"The only thing I can tell you is we think we had a great year," Miles said.

"This football team had as great a run as anybody in the country, playing eight nationally ranked teams. I think this team has accomplished a lot. I think that's for the voters to decide."

On Monday night, they did. And Alabama isn't sharing the 2011 national title with anyone.

HOW IT HAPPENED

By **MIKE HERNDON**

WHY ALABAMA WON

- Suffocating defense. The Crimson Tide held LSU to only 92 yards of total offense and did not allow the Tigers to cross midfield until midway through the fourth quarter. When Tide fans think about dominant defense now, they won't think of 1992. They won't think of 1978. They'll think of 2011.
- Key moment. Down 15-0, LSU drove to Alabama's 32 midway through the fourth quarter, its first and only foray into Tide territory. But DeQuan Menzie threw Michael Ford for a 3-yard loss, Jordan Jefferson threw two incomplete passes and Dont'a Hightower stripped the ball away from Jefferson on fourth down, with Nick Gentry recovering to end the threat and, essentially, the game.
- Three stars. 1.Courtney Upshaw. The senior linebacker was the biggest impact player on a defense full of them, leading the Tide with seven tackles and a sack. He was a frequent visitor to the LSU backfield. 2. Jeremy Shelley. After Alabama's special teams contributed to its downfall in the first meeting with LSU, Shelley made sure it wouldn't happen again. Typically the Tide's short-yardage kicker, Shelley took all seven of the Tide's attempts, a new record for any bowl game, and tied the record for made field goals with five. He was 2-of-4 from beyond 40 yards. 3. AJ McCarron. After his ability to lead the Tide to a title was questioned throughout the year, the sophomore from Mobile did just that – and did it in style. He completed 23 of 34 passes for 234 yards and, while he had no touchdowns, he also threw no interceptions.

WHERE'D HE COME FROM?

- When Marquis Maze pulled a hamstring on a 49-yard punt return in the first quarter, the Crimson Tide lost its top receiver for the rest of the game. Kevin Norwood filled the void, however, catching four passes for a game-high 78 yards, an average of 19.5 yards per catch.

ROUGH DAY

- Jordan Jefferson has made a lot of great memories at LSU, but his last game as a Tiger will be one he'd probably prefer to forget. He completed 11 of 17 passes for 53 yards and one interception, an ill-advised shovel pass that went straight to Alabama LB C.J. Mosley. He also ran for 15 yards on 14 attempts, a total that includes four sacks.

CALL OF THE DAY

- Alabama ran 30 first-down plays. Nineteen of them were passes. Four of the 11 first-down runs came in the fourth quarter, as Alabama started running clock with a 15-0 lead. Alabama coach Nick Saban said after the game that throwing on first down was a strategy his staff decided it didn't do often enough in the first meeting between the teams. "We knew we were going to have to throw the ball on first down to move the football offensively," he said.

WHAT FANS ARE SAYING

- Saban wouldn't say so – "I don't like to make comparisons," he said – but this could be the most dominant defense in Alabama history. Before Monday night's game, LSU coach Les Miles was getting questions about whether his team might be the best in college football history. After Monday, the only thing people are talking about is whether the Tide's defense is the best ever.

LOOKING AHEAD

- While Alabama revels in its second national title in the past three years, the only question now is how many of these Crimson Tide stars will return. Juniors Trent Richardson, Dre Kirkpatrick, Robert Lester and Dont'a Hightower all face decisions on whether to declare for the NFL draft or return for their senior year. Those decisions can wait, however. Monday night was a time for celebration.

Alabama's Brad Smelley is stopped by LSU defender
Ryan Baker in the first quarter.

PHOTO/BILL STARLING

ALABAMA BEATDOWN IS ONE FOR THE AGES

By **JON SOLOMON**

NEW ORLEANS – Alabama strength coach Scott Cochran engulfed defensive coordinator Kirby Smart in a bear hug on the field of the Superdome.

"Look at that!" Cochran screamed at Smart, pointing at the scoreboard. "That's a goose egg, baby!"

Alabama 21, LSU 0 wasn't just domination. It was a beatdown.

It was AJ McCarron brilliantly executing Jim McElwain's final game plan as Alabama offensive coordinator. It was Jeremy Shelley rising to the occasion with five field goals.

And as always, it was the Crimson Tide defense imposing its will on an opponent. You're free to start the debate now. No, not the split title talk. Where does this Alabama defense rank in college football history?

"I feel we're one of the greatest of all-time," safety Mark Barron said. "Hopefully we proved that to everybody else tonight. We have so many playmakers, such great chemistry. We didn't want to give up anything."

Alabama is the first team since Oklahoma in 1986 to lead the nation in fewest points allowed, rushing defense, passing defense and total defense. Alabama had the lowest scoring defense since Auburn in 1988 and the lowest total defense since Oklahoma in 1986.

There hadn't been a shutout in a national title game since Miami blanked Nebraska 22-0 at the 1992 Orange Bowl. Bizarrely, LSU acted as if it had the Cornhuskers' option offense and kept running an unimaginative game plan that was conducted ineptly by Jordan Jefferson.

"I thought they'd have more success with the speed option and they didn't," Smart said. "They didn't cut our corners, they didn't cut the guys on the perimeter. Once they couldn't cut them, they didn't have much success."

How bad was it that Les Miles stayed with Jefferson? Miles got badgered with this opening question in his news conference on why he didn't pull Jefferson for Jarrett Lee.

"Coach, did you ever consider bringing in Jarrett Lee, considering that you weren't taking any chances on the field? Now, I know Alabama's

defense is dominant. But come on, that's ridiculous, five first downs. ... I'll tell you from the fans' standpoint, how can you not maybe push the ball down the field and bring in Jarrett Lee? So what if you get a pick six?"

Even Smart said he kept waiting for Lee to replace Jefferson. Miles said he considered Lee but wanted someone who could handle the pass rush.

It wouldn't have mattered.

"We kept Jefferson in the pocket this time," linebacker Dont'a Hightower said. "We disguised some things and confused him."

When LSU finally crossed midfield in the fourth quarter for the first time, it felt like a touchdown for the Tigers. Alabama kept the SEC's domination upfront in the BCS Championship Game alive and well, only this time it came at the expense of a fellow SEC team.

LSU turned into Ohio State right before our eyes. Alabama held the Tigers to 92 total yards, the second fewest in a BCS bowl. Florida held Ohio State to 82 yards in the 2007 BCS Championship Game.

There's no doubting Alabama deserves this national championship. Forget the split national title talk.

"If you look at that first game, we really won it statistically but we fell short on the points," Barron said. "I think this proves we were the better team. We came into their house and beat them by three touchdowns."

The only debate left is where this Alabama defense ranks. Is it better than Alabama's '92 defense? Old-timers will say no. Stats might say otherwise.

That 2009 national title defense anchored by Rolando McClain, Terrence Cody and Javier Arenas? Former Alabama quarterback Greg McElroy believes 2011 was better.

"From a speed perspective, it's not even close. This one's better," McElroy said. "Granted, in '09, there were a lot of role players who really did a lot of special things. I know we wouldn't have won it if it weren't for the guys who made the sacrifice in '09. But at the same time, this defense just wanted to be the best and I really respect that. They went above and beyond what was ever expected of them."

Alabama's defense made its usual statement. Let the all-time debate begin.

C.A. McKnight and Daniel Freeman, both of Tuscaloosa, celebrate Alabama's fourth field goal against LSU.
PHOTO/JEFF ROBERTS

Alabama wide receiver Kevin Norwood hauls in a long pass past LSU cornerback Tyrann Mathieu.
PHOTO/MARK ALMOND

LSU wide receiver Rueben Randle is tackled by
Alabama defensive back Mark Barron.
PHOTO/MARK ALMOND

Alabama running back Trent Richardson is seen during warm-ups.
PHOTO/BILL STARLING

TV AUDIENCE WITNESSES TIDE'S DESTRUCTION OF LSU

By **DOUG SEGREST**

The Rematch of the Century proved to be a one-sided contest despite ESPN's weeklong hype and all-day buildup.

In terms of drama, in terms of the broadcast, ESPN couldn't capture the electricity Alabama and LSU provided CBS on Nov. 5. Despite playing in the enclosed Superdome, the fan noise didn't match the raucous, electric atmosphere of the Bryant-Denny Stadium original, when the intensity was palpable even from your couch.

Don't blame ESPN, and don't blame the veteran announcing team of Brent Musburger and Kirk Herbstreit.

Blame Alabama for taking all the air out of the building with a dominant BCS Championship Game performance. Herbstreit emphasized the point early in the fourth quarter as the cameras panned a dejected LSU sideline and lingered on cornerback Tyrann "Honey Badger" Mathieu.

"Alabama has just come after them and taken ... look at this – the attitude. I've never seen an LSU team look like this," Herbstreit said.

LSU trailed by only two touchdowns at the time, but in a series in which touchdowns are rare, neither of the announcers gave the Tigers a sliver of hope.

"This is a mauling, folks, a mauling," Musburger said minutes later.

And it was.

SOME OF THE HIGHLIGHTS
AND LOWLIGHTS
GOLD MOMENTS

• College GameDay set the pregame tone with features on Nick Saban's relationship with his late father at the dawn of his football career in West Virginia and Wright Thompson's melodic piece on LSU defensive back Mathieu. How do you sum up the game of the Honey Badger? Simply: "He plays jazz" on the field.

• ESPN captured visual images throughout the night that told the story without narrative, such as the shot of an LSU fan with a gold-and-purple mohawk and Alabama defensive end Jesse Williams decked out in war paint. But none matched the anguish on Marquis Maze's face at the start of the second half after he learned he was done for the night because of an injury.

• A couple of other images for Crimson Tide fans to treasure were Saban's relaxed smile after a Gatorade dousing and the postgame meeting with Les Miles, which was closer to heartfelt conversation than a typical handshake.

• Herbstreit played up the threat of LSU running the option and also pointed out quickly how Alabama took it away when defensive MVP Courtney Upshaw spoiled an early play, forcing Jordan Jefferson to pitch early, then chasing down the running back for a loss.

• Herbstreit also quickly pointed out how Alabama broke from tendencies by throwing on first down, rolling AJ McCarron out and utilizing receiver Darius Hanks out of the backfield. "I think LSU lost some of their aggression" as a result, Herbstreit said.

• With LSU having only one first down late in the opening half, Musburger and Herbstreit both noted the offensive confusion, starting with Jefferson. For Jefferson, the commentary would get worse.

• At halftime, Auburn's Gene Chizik pointed out why the LSU defense could be in bigger trouble in the second half due to the Crimson Tide's 41 first-half snaps, which wore down "the psyche of their defense. Right now they're not sure they can get off the field," Chizik said.

• Chizik also gave props to players who stepped up after the injury to Maze.

• When Jefferson panicked and threw an interception right into the

Alabama fans cheer the first points scored against LSU by Alabama in the BCS National Championship game as fans celebrate on the campus of the University of Alabama in Tuscaloosa. **PHOTO/JEFF ROBERTS**

hands of C.J. Mosley in the second half, Musburger spared no sympathy for the LSU quarterback, calling it "a horrible mistake."

• Erin Andrews finally got to the question every LSU fan wanted to ask after the game: Why didn't LSU go to backup Jarrett Lee? The speed of the Alabama rush, Miles replied.

GLITCHES

• There weren't many, but a key stat was missed after Maze's 49-yard punt return in the first quarter to set up the initial score. Coming into the game, LSU had allowed a total of six punt return yards combined, but Musburger and Herbstreit don't pick up on it right away. In fairness, Maze's game-ending injury proved more immediate.

• Musburger noted that Trent Richardson was not on the field early on, raising the specter of an injury. Richardson reappeared after a couple of series, but without explanation. After a hesitant run, he returned with a vengeance.

• Musburger flirted with blasphemy when he asked if Saban's two national titles would make fans forget Bear Bryant. Before ESPN could be bombarded with protests, Musburger corrected himself.

Alabama defenders Dont'a Hightower (30), Courtney Upshaw (41) and Xzavier Dickson (47) celebrate a play in the first quarter.
PHOTO/MIKE KITTRELL

McELWAIN'S PASSING PLAN PAYS OFF

By TOMMY HICKS

NEW ORLEANS – It started with Alabama's first play from scrimmage. That's when the offense showed its hand, when it let LSU and everyone else know what was coming.

Instead of handing the ball off to Heisman Trophy finalist Trent Richardson, offensive coordinator Jim McElwain put the ball – and the game plan – in the hands of quarterback AJ McCarron. The Mobile native was ready for the responsibility. On that first play from scrimmage, McCarron tossed a short pass to Brad Smelley that turned into a 15-yard gain. He then hit Smelley again on the next play for 4 yards. After a Richardson run, he completed a 6-yard pass to Michael Williams.

The drive would stall, but the plan did not. Short passes, especially on first down, opened up the Alabama offense and kept LSU's defense on its toes. It was a simple plan, but one that worked to perfection against the Tigers, triggering an offense that, although missing some touchdown opportunities, dominated the LSU defense.

It proved to be a championship plan; Alabama using McCarron, the game's Most Outstanding Offensive Player as its offensive trigger, dominated LSU en route to a convincing 21-0 victory over the Tigers for the BCS National Championship at a sold-out Mercedes-Benz Superdome.

To those watching the game, it appeared a genius approach and plan. To McElwain, it was more of the same.

"There was no reinventing the wheel," McElwain, who now heads to his new job as head coach at Colorado State, said. "I just thought the guys executed it. Obviously, we should have put more points on the board, but you know I've never been one to worry about anything but that final score, and the last time I checked, I think we won."

McCarron made it all click with his success throwing the football. He was 23-of-34 for 234 yards, no touchdowns and no interceptions. His accuracy on the short throws opened up the possibility of longer pass plays, which he also had some success in hitting. In turn, the passing game opened up the run and that opened up Alabama's

offense, one that produced five field goals and a late 34-yard scoring run by Richardson.

"I was very thankful first of all about it," McCarron said when he realized the game plan would be put, in large measure, on his shoulders. "We've been leaning on No. 3 (Richardson) all year. He's our workhorse, he's our main guy, and we knew coming into the game somebody else had to step up.

"Coach gave me an opportunity. When you've got a group of receivers like I have, it makes your job easy as the quarterback. You just have to put it in the air and let them go up and make plays

Alabama wide receiver Kevin Norwood makes a catch over LSU defender Tyrann Mathieu in the first quarter.
PHOTO/BILL STARLING

for you. They make plays that make you look like a hero. But it all goes back to those guys and that offensive line for giving me enough time." With LSU's primary defensive game plan established to stop Richardson, McCarron's task was to make plays. He did just that.

"I don't think I did anything special, really," McCarron said. "I mean, I always bust my butt in the film room. It helps when you got a little longer, you can study them a lot more. But I bust my butt in there, and I know everything they want to do – certain downs and distances. But that goes back to our coaching staff. We have the best coaching staff in the country.

"And, I mean, I felt like it was in my hands to kind of send Coach Mack off on a win, a big win, off to his new coaching journey. And, like I said, I'm just glad Coach gave me the opportunity. I don't think I did anything special, though. Like Coach always tells me, 'Just go out and play your

game.' On the bus ride the other day I sat with him. He just talked and he said, 'Listen, you don't have to win the game, just go play your game.' And I felt like I did that tonight."

His teammates felt he accomplished that goal. Offensive lineman Barrett Jones, the Outland Trophy winner, said, "AJ did a phenomenal job. He really did. He handled the pressure so well. He really was a cool customer. I really expected nothing less. He's fearless when he goes into games like this, and I think that was his best game of the year." Jones said when the game plan was first presented to the offense, he knew it was a plan built for success. "I don't think we finished drives as well as we wanted to, but as far as dominating the line of scrimmage, I think we did that," he said. "AJ had a lot of time, our running backs had a lot of space, and we really loved the ball well all night.

"Not trying to be cocky, but we really did (feel we could dominate). We totally missed a lot of opportunities in the first game, and we felt that we could capitalize on them this game." Seven players caught at least one McCarron pass. Smelley was his favorite target, catching seven passes for 39 yards, with Darius Hanks catching five passes for 58 and Kevin Norwood hauling in four for 78 yards. Brandon Gibson couldn't hold on to a pass that might have been good for a touchdown, but for the most part, the Crimson Tide offense moved the ball consistently and made plays, including 21 first downs.

"He did the things he needed to do to put points on the board, and as a defense we didn't do the things we needed to do to stop that," said LSU defensive back Eric Reid, who made the interception at the goal line in the first meeting of the teams that helped preserve the Tigers' win.

A motivated, emotional McCarron, who claimed the No. 3 spot on Alabama's single-season record for completions with 210 this season, made the plays that LSU counterpart Jordan Jefferson didn't make Monday night. McElwain said it was the right call.

"I thought AJ played well, but he's a good player," McElwain said. "I think his ceiling is way high. We're going to see a lot of football out of AJ McCarron. He's a sponge. ... He loves to learn and do anything he can to win ball games."

LSU running back Kenny Hilliard is wrapped up by Alabama linebacker Jerrell Harris and linebacker Dont'a Hightower.
PHOTO/MARK ALMOND

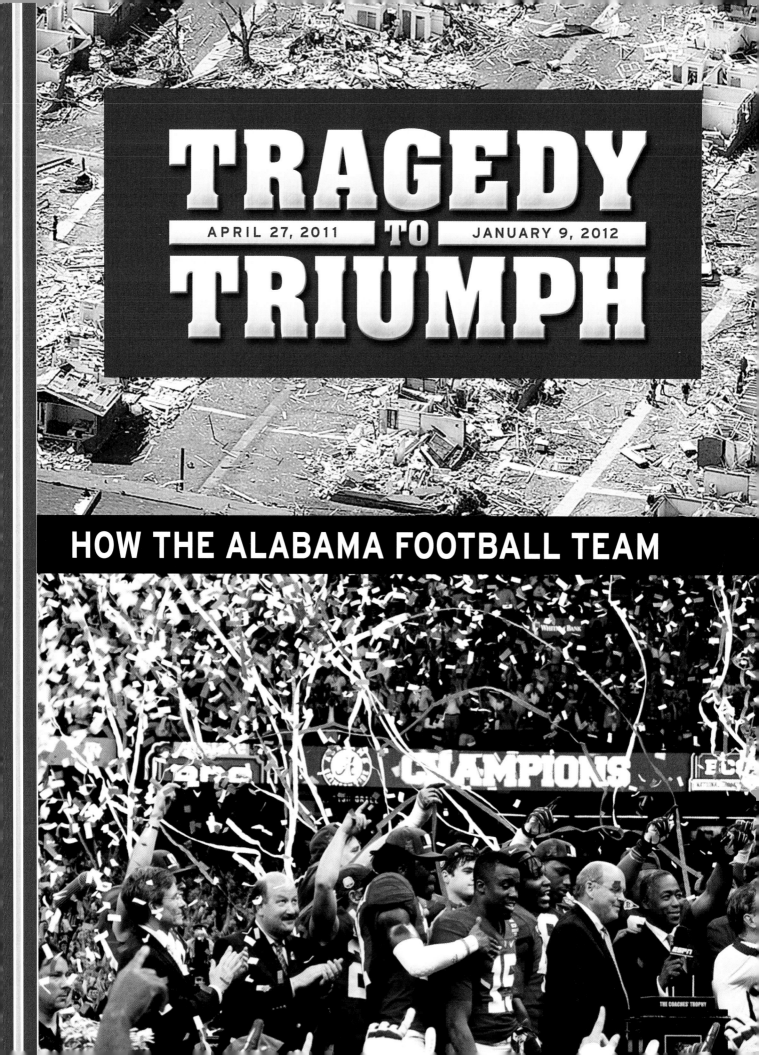

TRAGEDY

APRIL 27, 2011 **TO** **JANUARY 9, 2012**

TRIUMPH

HOW THE ALABAMA FOOTBALL TEAM

HELPED LIFT A COMMUNITY

MILE-WIDE TWISTER LEAVES TUSCALOOSA IN RUBBLE

By **IZZY GOULD** and
DON KAUSLER, JR.

TUSCALOOSA — At least 15 people were killed and more than 100 injured as severe weather barreled through Tuscaloosa Wednesday afternoon, and that total is expected to grow as rescuers continue to dig the city out of the rubble today.

Pearline Gilbert Hinton and her son, Kendrell Dewayne Hinton, feared they might be among the victims as they gathered in their small bathroom hoping to dodge death.

The 54-year-old mother climbed in her bathtub. Her 16-year-old son said he prayed to God as he hugged a toilet.

"I was just saying 'Jesus, Jesus, Jesus,'" Hinton said. "I was just praising the Lord and that thing was just coming."

Outside, a deadly tornado was sweeping across their 10th Avenue apartment complex.

Tuscaloosa Mayor Walt Maddox confirmed the deaths and injury toll late Wednesday.

"I fear both of those numbers are going to grow," he said.

The storm roared east across Interstate 359, leaving a swath of damage that closed portions of the highway and caused traffic jams on secondary roads.

Many cars at Townsend BMW had their windows blown out. Debris littered parking lots and streets. Power lines were knocked down, and portions of roofs were ripped open. The Salvation Army building on 29th Street was gutted.

Gary Lewis, who has owned and operated the Rama Jama's restaurant on Paul W. Bryant Drive next to Bryant-Denny Stadium for the past 16 years, described the storm's arrival.

"When I got there, it just didn't seem real. I looked out my door

over here on the west side next to Bryant-Denny Stadium and debris was flying. I thought, 'Oh, my God! It's here,'" he said. "One of my cashiers took cover under a booth, but it wasn't here. It was a few miles from here. I was just seeing the edges of it. It's the first time I've seen a tornado."

Fortunately for Rama Jama, but unfortunately for others, the storm turned toward 15th Street, Lewis said. Later, he went to the area and called the damage "total devastation."

"Everything I saw was gone. McAllister's, major damage. No Taco Casa, no McDonald's, Mike and Ed's Barbeque, major damage. All those houses on that little lake are splintered. Contemporary Mitsubishi, major damage . . . what I saw just didn't seem real," he said. "This could be the most terrible thing that's happened to Tuscaloosa."

Maddox, at a Wednesday night news conference, said the situation has overwhelmed city resources.

"We have to be cognizant of the fact that what we faced today was massive damage on a scale that we haven't seen in Tuscaloosa in quite some time," the mayor said. "It is going to require every available resource in the city to deal with this matter. . . . We're not talking about a matter of hours, a matter of days. We're talking about a matter of months in this recovery effort."

Rescue operations were to continue through the night Wednesday, and the National Guard also was expected to arrive.

"We still have people trapped in their homes. We still have reports of gas leaks throughout the city. We've got the grim responsibility now of dealing with fatalities," Maddox said. "Everybody that can stay home and stay off the streets are helping their fellow neighbor. Please, please, do not get on the roads for at least the next 24 hours."

Damage estimates from the storm will likely reach into the millions of dollars, he said.

At the complex where Hinton, who huddled in the bathroom with her son, lived, hundreds of people walked through rubble as gas leaked from pipes, and water sprayed from some of the leveled homes. Some of the injured begged for help, while others stared in horror and disbelief.

In one home, men gathered atop rubble that once had been a home and collectively lifted and tossed wreckage from atop a 6-year-old boy. Once he was freed, firefighters checked his vital signs and placed him on a wooden door they used as a gurney.

His shirtless, injured father wept before his son was taken to an ambulance that already held two more of the injured.

Hinton stood in the street in front of her home in a blue dress with no shoes and minor cuts on her feet. Her hair was cluttered with tiny pieces of insulation, but she and her son were grateful to be alive.

A firefighter approached Hinton and asked if she was familiar

Tuscaloosa after the tornado. **PHOTO/IZZY GOULD**

enough with the neighborhood to help match names with homes. He quickly went to find shoes for her, retrieving a cowboy boot and another shoe that was not hers. The gesture was enough to bring a smile to Hinton's face.

Behind her was a row of cars that were once parallel parked on her street. They now sat on her yard including her totaled 1998 Buick LeSabre, which was trapped beneath a wrecked Dodge Durango.

The windows and roof in Hinton's apartment, 2B, were completely removed, providing a clear view to the sky.

"I had been watching the news and I seen it coming, and I told my son

to, 'Come on, let's get in the bathroom,'" Hinton said. "We got in there and everything just started crashing and breaking, chairs and everything were flying. I mean TVs and cars and everything."

As afternoon turned to night and more people filled the streets, a dose of reality hit Hinton.

Where would she go? What would she do?

"I'm trying to call my siblings. Ain't nobody picking up," Hinton said. "I ain't got nowhere to go."

(Below) Funnel cloud strikes Tuscaloosa, on Wednesday, April 27, 2011. This photo was taken looking north from Taylorsville. PHOTO/DON KAUSLER, JR.

TORNADO PUTS SPORTS IN PROPER PERSPECTIVE

By **JON SOLOMON**

Thursday was supposed to be a triumphant day for the state of Alabama in the sports world.

All those crystal balls and Heisman trophies from the past two years gave Alabama and Auburn multiple first-round NFL Draft picks in the same year for the first time.

But it feels so meaningless now.

The draft, the games, the trophies, the bragging rights – they're all diversions from our everyday lives until real life wreaks unimaginable devastation on far, far too many people.

Your heart aches for those affected by Wednesday's tornadoes in Alabama. The accounts keep pouring in of death and destruction.

Loved ones are missing. Photos and names get posted on TV and websites as family members desperately search for them. They're the kinds of pleas we're used to seeing elsewhere, not here.

This is our Katrina.

We will get through this – slowly, eventually, together. But it's brutal to watch, from Cullman to Tuscaloosa, from Pleasant Grove to Pratt City, and from so many other areas, some of which we might not fully know about yet.

Whether your team won or lost, you will never forget how you felt when Auburn rallied from 24 down to stun Alabama at Bryant-Denny Stadium. But my goodness, that tornado bearing down on Bryant-Denny on Wednesday will be forever etched in your mind, knowing that the destructive path it was taking would never allow some people to recover.

Not surprisingly, a Facebook page called "Toomer's for Tuscaloosa" quickly emerged with Auburn fans supporting recovery efforts in Tuscaloosa. It's the spin-off of "Tide for Toomer's," in which Alabama fans raised money for Auburn's damaged oak trees.

The hidden truth about the Alabama-Auburn rivalry becomes clear during trying times such as this: The vast majority of the teams' fans aren't certifiably insane, nor do they spend their time trying to dig up dirt on the other side.

How inconsequential do the Brent Calloway and Auburn NCAA investigation stories feel now? What wouldn't we give to have those conversations today instead of sifting through rubble and bodies?

The NFL Draft represents a culmination of the unprecedented football success seen in this state during the past two years. Yet some draftees from the state, especially those who lived and played in Tuscaloosa, understandably carried a heavy heart in New York.

Former Alabama quarterback Greg McElroy tweeted: "A day that is supposed to be filled with excitement has been slapped with a realization of what really matters. Very sobering."

"im amazed at the damage the tornado has done," former Alabama running back Mark Ingram posted on Twitter. "i wish i could do something but im sending my heart and prayers out to everyone in bama!"

Sports will eventually assist our state's recovery, as only sports can do when senseless things happen. Diversion is the real role of sports – nothing more, nothing less.

Just as the New York Yankees briefly diverted minds away from 9/11 and the New Orleans Saints provided a diversion after Hurricane Katrina, so too will Alabama and Auburn football. It will inspire people in this state in a new way, as odd as that sounds for a state that already takes worshipping football heroes to extremes.

But today, those moments of diversion seem so far away. Today, football has never felt so insignificant in Alabama.

A crew paints a houndstooth ribbon on the football field of Bryant-Denny Stadium in remembrance of the victims and damage the tornadoes caused that ripped through Tuscaloosa last spring. Preparations were under way for the first football game of the season against Kent State. PHOTO/MICHELLE CAMPBELL

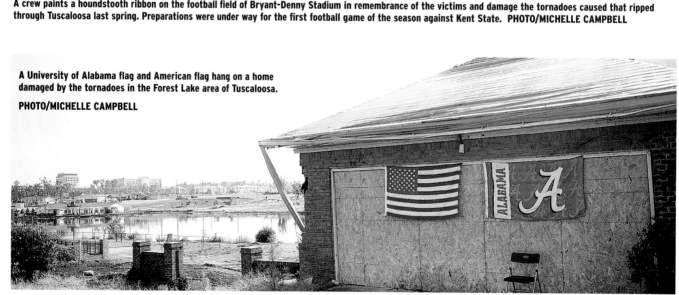

A University of Alabama flag and American flag hang on a home damaged by the tornadoes in the Forest Lake area of Tuscaloosa.

PHOTO/MICHELLE CAMPBELL

SABAN VISITS SHELTER AMID VAST DESTRUCTION IN TUSCALOOSA

By IZZY GOULD

Nick Saban emerged from a police car Friday afternoon along with his wife at a shelter that was housing and feeding roughly 700 displaced residents.

It was the second visit in as many days for Alabama's head football coach. This day, he signed autographs while those with ties to the University of Alabama helped pass out food and Crimson Tide clothing inside the Belk Activity Center, which is being utilized by the American Red Cross.

Volunteers here came all the way from California just hours after a tornado shredded a path just south of the university's campus. Saban said he has not seen anything like this, the devastation strewn across a defined section of Tuscaloosa stretching northeast.

Saban, who is often the figure people look to for guidance, offered a stern statement.

"For those of you who don't respect the warnings of weather and how it can affect you, you need to look at this," Saban said. "I'll never again not respect some siren to get out of the thunder and lightning, hurricane warning, tornado warning, whatever it is. This was the real deal."

Saban broke plans to appear on the NFL Network as a guest analyst for the NFL Draft this weekend. He did attend the opening round of the draft Thursday night in New York where Alabama had four players selected in the first round, a first for the program.

Saban said he was compelled to return to Tuscaloosa in the wake of the destruction, and praised the local response.

"The community spirit has been wonderful," Saban said. "I was really proud of the way the university responded. The students as well as our team, you can't just be a team on Saturday. You have to be a team in the worst of times. This is the worst of times for a lot of people."

In terms of Alabama football players, Saban said many of them helped hand out water and food. Only one player had been injured in the tornado - Carson Tinker, who suffered a concussion. His girlfriend, Ashley Harrison, was killed when the tornado struck his house near the Tuscaloosa campus.

> **"You can't just be a team on Saturday. You have to be a team in the worst of times. This is the worst of times for a lot of people."**
>
> *Coach Nick Saban*

Saban said most of the team was expected to return home, now that finals have been canceled and the semester finished.

"Everybody's doing fine," Saban said. "Our team, we had one guy that was injured. He's stable and doing well, out of the hospital. We've had quite a few guys involved with what is going on here the last couple of days, but I think after today, most of our players will leave."

President Obama walks with Alabama Gov. Robert Bentley through the storm damage in Tuscaloosa. **PHOTO/JOE SONGER**

(Above and Left) Children in The Preserve neighborhood in Hoover, sell lemonade, cookies, coffee, brownies, tea and accept donations of non-perishable food items, clothing, blankets, toiletries, money, water, etc. for relief of the Tuscaloosa tornado victims Sunday, May 1, 2011. They are calling their effort the "Tuscaloosa Relief Kitchen." Tori Botthof (4) is shown in her "Help Tuscaloosa" T-shirt with her favorite doll which she is donating to the cause.

PHOTO/JEFF ROBERTS

SPORTS HAS ITS ROLE IN AFTERMATH OF STORMS

By **MARK McCARTER**

The storms have stopped some of the games.

They haven't stopped those who play them.

From across the state, indeed from across the country, come countless feel-good stories involving coaches and athletes and organizations pitching in for tornado relief.

The help ranges from the New York Yankees to Anthony Grant, from Talladega Superspeedway to the Auburn football team.

It's a well-worn cliche in times of disaster that "it puts things in perspective" when it comes to the frivolity of sports.

Clearly, sports teams and sports figures are taking serious roles in leadership and assistance in helping recover from Wednesday's devastating tornado outbreak.

For instance:

- Auburn football players, coaches and other personnel have helped in clean-up operations in Cullman and Pleasant Grove. Coach Gene Chizik reportedly wanted to keep the news quiet, so it didn't come across as some publicity-seeking move.
- The New York Yankees announced they are donating $500,000 to the relief effort – half going to the Red Cross, half to the Salvation Army.
- The St. Louis Blues hockey team is contributing $20,000 to the Red Cross.
- The Buffalo Bills, who drafted former Alabama player Marcell Dareus in the first round and whose general manager Buddy Nix is an Alabama native, have teamed with Verizon Wireless to donate $10,000 to the American Red Cross.
- The Southeastern Conference, which has donated more than $1 million to disaster relief in the past, has issued a statement encouraging fans to donate to the Red Cross.
- Talladega Superspeedway has committed $100,000 to the American Red Cross and offered an intriguing way for race fans to pitch in. Between May 6-8, for a $50 donation, fans may drive their personal vehicles around the speedway.
- The Huntsville Stars have been serving meals through their concession stand. They've been available at a nominal cost, though first-responders, power crews and other emergency workers are being fed for free.
- Alabama basketball coach Anthony Grant, who has been joined by his staff in distributing supplies in Tuscaloosa, has created a fund at Bryant Bank called the "Sweet Home Fund" to aid families hit by the tornadoes.
- Alabama football coach Nick Saban has been making visits to shelters in Tuscaloosa to encourage those displaced from their homes.

Remember how Alabama fans leapt to support Auburn fans who were so angered by the poisoning of the oak trees at Toomer's Corner?

A Facebook page called "Tide for Toomer's" was created, raising money to help save the trees.

Now, there is a new Facebook page: "Toomer's for Tuscaloosa."

Its organizers dispatched four trucks full of supplies and ice to Tuscaloosa on Saturday, with items donated by Auburn fans.

What a way to put the Alabama-Auburn rivalry in the proper perspective.

(Above) Former Alabama football star Javier Arenas, standing in the middle, and friends spread out items that he brought back from Kansas City, Mo., to be donated to Tuscaloosa tornado victims.
PHOTO/DON KAUSLER, JR.

Students from Auburn University and the University of Alabama join forces in storm relief through the House United Habitat Project. The students, with help from Habitat for Humanity volunteers, are building two homes on 5th Street NE in the Holt Community of Tuscaloosa for two families that lost their homes to the April 27th tornado. One of the homes is being rebuilt for the Teddy Rowe family and the other home is for a family that will be chosen this week. Sixty Alabama students and 30 Auburn students are helping build the two Habitat homes. Students work in the attic of the Teddy Rowe family home. PHOTO/JOE SONGER

FOOTBALL HELPS TIDE'S TINKER HEAL EMOTIONS

By **DON KAUSLER, JR.**

Most of what's going to heal has healed.

The gashes in his head are gone. The concussion is history. The broken bone in his right wrist is mended. The large cut on his right ankle now is just a little scratch that might leave a big scar.

But that will be nothing compared to the nasty scar on Carson Tinker's emotions.

How exactly does one heal from the unspeakable tragedy of a killer tornado that ravaged Tuscaloosa on April 27?

From a closet inside the house he shared with two others, Alabama's junior deep snapper was blown 100 yards into an empty field across the street. As the house crumbled, his girlfriend, Ashley Harrison, was ripped from his firm grasp. Her body was found in the same field the next morning.

"When those kind of things happen, they don't just go away," Alabama coach Nick Saban said. "You have to learn how to deal with them, and he's done a pretty good job of that."

Thank goodness for football. It has been Tinker's therapy.

"Oh, yeah, football," he said, breaking into a grin in the Alabama media room, where he agreed to appear if he wasn't asked to rehash his painful day. "The people I've known from football, we're just a family up here. You really can't explain the relief that I get from this."

Somebody recently asked the returning starter from Murfreesboro, Tenn., how the coaches have been treating him.

"I said, 'The same exact way. Nothing is different coming out here. They're not feeling sorry for me,'" he said. "That's the most therapeutic thing. I mean I haven't been doing bad, but they always demand your very best. And it is comforting to know you're out there getting yelled at. I guess that sounds weird."

Can any Alabama player possibly be looking more forward to the season-opening game a week from today against Kent State?

"I was telling somebody earlier. They asked what Sept. 3 meant to me," Tinker said. "I said, 'I've been looking forward to that day for a very long time.' Not just the day. The season. Every day I've been working to get ready for the season, and it's here, and I'm ready. You know what I mean? You can't put into words how that feels."

Alabama long snapper Carson Tinker, along with the teammates, wears a houndstooth ribbon to remember the April 27 tornado and No. 77 for fellow teammate Aaron Douglas who passed away, during an NCAA college football game against Kent State in Tuscaloosa. Tinker's girlfriend was killed when a tornado struck Tuscaloosa on April 27, 2011. Now, as the Crimson Tide prepares to play in the BCS championship against top-ranked LSU on Monday night, the healing continues in Tuscaloosa.

AP PHOTO/BUTCH DILL

Alabama snapper Carson Tinker is shown in the second quarter of the North Texas game at Bryant-Denny Stadium.

PHOTO/MARK ALMOND

He can try.

"When I was doing my rehab and doing all the things that I needed to get healthy, what I thought about was running out of that tunnel and playing football," Tinker said.

He had to walk before he could run.

"I remember I came back, and I couldn't run yet, but everybody else was out there running," Tinker said of summer conditioning sessions. "I was just out there with them. . . . It was very encouraging and inspiring to me to see them out there working hard and getting ready for the season.

"I knew that I had to be out there, and I wanted to be out there. I started running again around the first of July."

Saban is impressed with Tinker's perseverance.

"If you're around Carson, he's such a positive and upbeat guy," Saban said. "You really don't know that anything happened. He's probably handled this as well as anybody could."

Spring graduation was postponed until early August. Harrison would have received her diploma that day. Her family from Texas made the trip.

"I think this graduation was something that brought some thoughts back for him that were

A make shift memorial to Ashley Therese Perret Harrison (1/10/89-4/27/11) at one of the Tuscaloosa tornado sites. PHOTO/IZZY GOULD

hard for him to deal with," Saban said. "He's going to have to continue to sort of persevere. That's a tough thing."

Three wooden crosses now stand in the field where Tinker used to hit golf balls across 25th Street from the house that now is just a lot with little debris remaining. One cross memorializes

Harrison. A folding metal chair, painted red, faces the cross, on and around which people have left items in her honor.

The other simple crosses stand nearby, where Tinker's and Harrison's dogs are buried. A short golf club leans against one cross. Leashes are wrapped around the other one. On top of the grave are 20 golf balls and several dog-food dishes.

It is a stirring scene to remember from a day to forget.

Teammates, coaches and others have helped Tinker cope. Fans have sent letters and emails.

"People I haven't talked to in years have called me," Tinker said. "At the same time, people who give me support, I try to give back.

"Dr. (Kevin) Elko, who comes to talk to us, says, 'Some people pray for blessings, but I pray that I can be a blessing for somebody.' I do. I want to go out and I want to reach everybody that I can and try to inspire them, because I mean there's a lot of people that have been through very similar things that I've been through, and if I can help them, I'm all for it."

Tuscaloosa residents filled Government Plaza to take part in the Spirit of Tuscaloosa Candlelight Vigil, Wednesday June 1, 2011. The vigil was held to honor those lost to the April 27th tornado that ravaged the city and killed 43. PHOTO/JOE SONGER

Rosedale Courts, 10th and Greensboro Avenues. PHOTO/IZZY GOULD

OPENER MINDFUL OF APRIL 27

Signs of damage remain.

By **IZZY GOULD**

TUSCALOOSA — The last time automobiles inched bumper-to-bumper along McFarland Boulevard, Alabama was not playing football.

The almost weekly traffic jam in the fall is an indicator – the Crimson Tide is about to kick off.

RVs with Alabama flags again rolled across these streets Friday afternoon as fans began to fill the city.

Most are here to cheer another promising season for the second-ranked Tide. Today is the season opener against Kent State, Nick Saban's alma mater.

The days following April 27 and the tornado that plowed through neighborhoods just south of campus – one of many tornadoes across the South that day – attracted people from across the country. There were volunteers, curiosity seekers, celebrities, reporters, even

President Barack Obama toured the damage.

There were countless searches for the missing. Cadaver dogs tip-toed through seemingly endless debris, nosing through the rubble. Families literally picked through the pieces of what had been their homes. They looked for clothing, photographs and prized possessions.

When fans converge on Tuscaloosa this morning they can easily find signs of the EF4 monster that haunts the dreams of many to this day. Cars still move through the commu-

Alabama Gov. Robert Bentley, far right, was on hand to thank local law enforcement and emergency service employees during pregame activity at the Kent State game at Bryant Denny Stadium. PHOTO/GLENN BAESKE

nity with windows blown out since that historic afternoon. Gutted homes still stand as they did after Mother Nature's violence, though many have been demolished and some rebuilding has begun.

"I think it still shocks me every time you drive on 15th Street," Tide junior Barrett Jones said. "That's what always gets me every time I drive by there, I'm still a little surprised by it. I guess I should be used to it by now, and at some point I am. I think this is something we don't need to forget about. . . . I think a lot of guys are excited about the game this Saturday and just getting our city back together. We kind of felt like that's when our city is all in one place on game days."

There will be symbols throughout Bryant-Denny Stadium showing Alabama's support to a community that idolizes its football program.

Houndstooth ribbons – symbolizing recovery from the tornado – will be painted on the field. Saban said players will wear similar ribbons on their helmets.

There will be a pregame salute to first re-

sponders on April 27, and likely other gestures throughout the day.

Of course, there will be a constant national attention as visitors retell the story through websites and television reports.

"We're very excited to open the season for a lot of different reasons," Saban said. ". . . Also, for the sake of our community from the standpoint of giving people, from a spiritual standpoint, something else to think about, something else to be passionate about, something else to create hope about. Also to continue to create awareness for the community that a lot of people are going to come to the game and see Tuscaloosa for the first time. Maybe that will inspire some people to continue to try to help rebuild our community."

Throughout the game, fans will be looking for answers about Alabama's highly hyped quarterback competition between AJ McCarron and Phillip Sims.

They will look at offensive left tackle where Jones will start, and true freshman Cyrus Kouand-

jio will try to win the job. Some will be reminded of another tragedy, the unexpected death of Aaron Douglas, who was competing for the spot in the spring.

Fans are anticipating a tuneup for next week's trip to Penn State. Alabama is favored by more than 30 points, and the defense has been compared to some of the Tide's best.

At the end of the day, what arguably will be most significant in retrospect is how this game helped with the next step in rebuilding lives.

Many look for hope in various ways. In Alabama, they look to a football game as a way to endure.

"We do feel somewhat of a responsibility and excitement just to get back on the field and to kind of bring this city back together," Jones said. "That's when probably the most people from the city are in one place is on game day. So were excited about getting back together and hopefully passing out some smiles."

Alabama defensive back DeQuan Menzie (24) and linebacker Courtney Upshaw (41) celebrate victory against Kent State.

PHOTO/MARK ALMOND

Alabama linebacker Dont'a Hightower works out during preseason NCAA college football drills on Sunday, Aug. 7, 2011. PHOTO/JASON HARLESS

LISTEN UP! Tide seems to be paying more attention to Saban this year.

By **DON KAUSLER, JR.**

TUSCALOOSA – Alabama coach Nick Saban speaks. His players hear. But do they listen? Do they absorb? Do they act?

They didn't in 2010. Saban repeatedly but unsuccessfully hammered a single, simple message. Practice and play to a high standard, he said. Blah, blah, blah, they heard. Don't focus on results, he said. Yak, yak, yak, they heard.

Ears received. Words were not perceived. The point was not believed.

As a result, a team that was coming off a national championship lost three games. A team that was ranked No. 1 in the preseason fell far short of expectations.

Now a new season nearly is upon the Crimson Tide, which is ranked No. 2 in both major preseason polls.

Will the results improve?

Listen up. There's evidence now that Saban's pupils might have been paying attention after all. Preseason practices have been distinctly different.

"It's a lot more intense," defensive back Will Lowery said. "We're out to prove something this year. Last year, everybody was kind of just throwing everything on us. 'Oh, you're going to be so great.' I know people are trying to do that this year."

Lowery then quoted his coach.

"'It's not about what you can do. It's what you do,'" Lowery said, repeating Saban's mantra. "He said last year we kind of bought into what we could do. That's what the team was about. This year, we're all about going out and proving it. We've been really grinding, really working this camp."

Now hear this. Saban has seemed distinctly different in the weeks leading to this season kick-off compared to a year ago, when the hard-to-please coach so often sounded agitated.

- "We have lots of guys committed to a high standard and have worked hard," he said on Aug. 7.
- "Yesterday, we probably had the best two practices in a day that we've had," he said on Aug. 16. "I really like the way the players responded to making the corrections that we needed to make from the scrimmage. We've made some progress."
- "The practices have been good," he said on Aug. 18. "The tempo has been good. We continue to make improvements."

Questions remain. Who will be the quarterback? Will underproven AJ McCarron and unproven Phillip Sims share the job? Who will catch the passes besides senior wide receivers Marquis Maze and Darius Hanks?

But the makings for a balanced offense are there. Star running back Trent Richardson and a veteran offensive line will provide the punch.

Ten starters are back from a defense that was young but talented last season. Senior linebackers Dont'a Hightower and Courtney Upshaw and senior safety Mark Barron bring play-making and leadership to a unit that was stout statistically last season.

During the offseason, a buzzword quickly bubbled up for a team that blew a 24-0 lead and lost to Auburn 28-27 last season.

"Our focus this year is finishing," senior nose guard Josh Chapman said on the first day of preseason camp. "That's one thing we want to do on the practice field. It kind of carries over into the game. We didn't finish a lot of times in practice. That's what we've got to do now. It starts now."

Alabama Coach Nick Saban instructs Alabama defensive back DeQuan Menzie during the first practice session of the season in Tuscaloosa, Ala., Friday, Aug. 5, 2011. PHOTO/JASON HARLESS

TIDE 48 GOLDEN FLASHES 7

Alabama wide receiver Marquis
Maze hauls in a 24-yard touchdown
pass from Alabama quarterback AJ
McCarron in the first quarter.

PHOTO/MARK ALMOND

Alabama running back Eddie Lacy leaps over Alabama offensive lineman Anthony Steen for extra yardage in the first quarter.

PHOTO/MARK ALMOND

GRADING THE TIDE

OFFENSE

C

Take away 4 giveaways and the offense was OK. How do you knock 482 yards and 48 points? Four interceptions were a major flaw.

DEFENSE

A

How often does a defense hold a foe to less than 100 yards? Kent State had 90, along with only six first downs.

SPECIAL TEAMS

B

DeAndrew White's fumble on a punt return was the lone blemish. Marquis Maze had 10 returns for 135 yards.

COACHING

A

QB competition was handled sensibly with more passes called than runs. Sixty-nine players were used. What can you criticize?

OVERALL

B

Room for improvement, but a decent start for a good team that can be great.

Assessment by Don Kausler, Jr.

McCARRON, MAZE LEAD ROUT

Alabama Helped to Restore a Sense of Normalcy in This Town Simply by Playing Football.

By **IZZY GOULD**

TUSCALOOSA — The second-ranked Crimson Tide disposed of Kent State 48-7, using the season opener to unveil a quarterback competition between AJ McCarron and Phillip Sims, though their performances were largely upstaged by the Tide's stout defense.

Pregame ceremonies at Bryant-Denny Stadium reminded fans of the tragic offseason since the Crimson Tide last hosted an opponent here.

Gov. Robert Bentley shook hands with first responders to the April 27 tornadoes that wrecked many parts of the South, including Tuscaloosa. Two houndstooth ribbons were painted on the field as symbols of the recovery effort.

There was a Roll Tide salute to the parents of Aaron Douglas, a former Alabama lineman who died during the offseason.

And, finally, there was football.

McCarron and Sims were the headliners, and they began their auditions for the starting job. Those performances will be dissected for the next week as fans and pundits debate whether the Crimson Tide has found its man to start at Penn State.

How did Alabama coach Nick Saban see it play out?

"AJ having played a little bit more probably played with a little more poise today. But we have a lot of confidence in Phillip and in most cases he plays extremely well."

McCarron, a sophomore, finished 14-for-23 passing for 226 yards, a touchdown and two interceptions. He guided five scoring drives, including a 24-yard touchdown pass to Marquis Maze for a 14-0 lead in the first quarter.

Maze dazzled with 253 all-purpose yards, including a game-high eight catches for 118 yards and the touchdown.

Sims, a freshman, went 7-for-14 passing for 73 yards, no touchdowns and two interceptions. Sims guided three scoring drives, but he was sacked twice and fumbled once.

Saban implemented his plan to have McCarron lead three series followed by Sims with three. The cycle repeated until Sims threw back-to-back interceptions on his first two drives of the second half.

The second one was intercepted by Sidney Saulter, whose 37-yard return reached the Tide's 3-yard line. Two plays later, quarterback Spencer Keith found Justin Thompson for a Kent State touchdown to pull within 24-7.

"The offense, we have their back," safety Mark Barron said. "We weren't upset with them about that. Of course, we wanted to keep that zero on the board, but at the same time things happen."

While Alabama (1-0) amassed 482 yards of offense led by three Trent Richardson touchdowns and one each from fellow running backs Eddie Lacy and Jalston Fowler, the defense limited the Golden Flashes (0-1) to 90 yards of offense and just six first downs.

> ## "We've got our defensive goals. Keep the offense to 13 or less points. We met our goal. We're pleased, but we're not satisfied."
> *Linebacker Dont'a Hightower*

The Tide was led by 10 tackles from true freshman Trey Depriest, and seven tackles each from linebackers Courtney Upshaw and Dont'a Hightower. C.J. Mosley and Quinton Dial had two of Alabama's four sacks, and Phelon Jones grabbed an interception.

If there was any cause for concern it was those four interceptions and four fumbles (one turned over). That's something to fret about with the Nittany Lions ahead.

"Offensively, at times we played well but never really looked crisp and sharp," Saban said. "Turnovers are critical. You've got to do a much, much better job of taking care of the ball."

AP TOP 10	1	2	3	4	5	6	7	8	9	10
09.04.11	OKLAHOMA	LSU	ALABAMA	BOISE ST.	FLORIDA ST.	STANFORD	TEXAS A&M	WISCONSIN	OK. ST.	NEBRASKA

Alabama running back Trent Richardson stretches past Kent State linebacker Luke Batton to score a first-quarter touchdown.

PHOTO/MARK ALMOND

TIDE DEFENSE IS MORE THAN GOOD ENOUGH

By DON KAUSLER, JR.

TUSCALOOSA — The statistics shouted. The players shrugged. Alabama's defense dominated Saturday, the statistics said.

"It wasn't perfect," free safety Mark Barron said. "We had some mistakes out there. I feel like we came out and had a good day, but it wasn't perfect."

In a 48-7 season-opening victory at Bryant-Denny Stadium, the Crimson Tide held Kent State to 90 total yards. Only Chattanooga (84, in 2009) has gained fewer yards on an Alabama defense in coach Nick Saban's five years.

The Tide allowed only six first downs. It forced eight three-and-outs on Kent State's first nine possessions.

The defense probably would have pitched a shutout if a Kent State interception had not been returned to Alabama's 3-yard line in the third quarter.

"You always don't want anybody to score," Alabama star linebacker Dont'a Hightower said. "We've got our defensive goals. Keep the offense to 13 or less points. We met our goal.

"We're pleased, but we're not satisfied. We'll get in the film room, get situated and see what happened, where we were wrong."

The Tide goes into games with many goals on defense.

"Holding the run to 3 yards," Hightower said. Kent State averaged 0.39 yards per rush as they netted 9 yards on 23 carries. The Golden Flashes averaged 1.2 yards per play.

"It's something that we pride ourselves on," Hightower said of achieving goals. "That's what's going to make us a great defense."

A shutout would have been nice, outside linebacker Courtney Upshaw said.

"We wanted it, but we've got to move on," he said. "We were backed up. We've just got to go out and dominate, no matter what the score is. We just want to play good, play hard every game, every snap."

The Tide forced only one turnover – a Phelon Jones interception – and did not force any fumbles despite emphasis on that skill during preseason practices. It had four sacks and three other tackles for a loss.

In other words, there is room for improvement.

"We can pick up a lot more things, technique wise and finishing – get more turnovers," Upshaw said.

The pressure now is up to the offense to play at the same level.

"We've got to live up to the standard of defense," running back Trent Richardson said. "They played good ball today. We've got to back them up. They can't do it by themselves. We've got to step our game up."

Alabama defensive back DeQuan Menzie and linebacker Courtney Upshaw team up to sack Kent State quarterback Spencer Keith in the first quarter.

PHOTO/MARK ALMOND

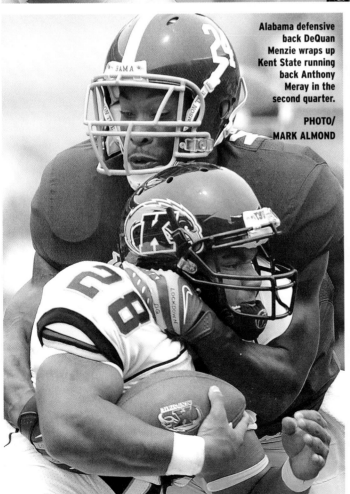

Alabama defensive back DeQuan Menzie wraps up Kent State running back Anthony Meray in the second quarter.

PHOTO/ MARK ALMOND

	1	2	3	4	FINAL
ALABAMA	21	3	14	10	48
KENT STATE	0	0	7	0	7

TOTAL YARDS

ALABAMA **482**

KENT STATE **90**

PASSING YARDS

ALABAMA **299**

KENT STATE **99**

RUSHING YARDS

ALABAMA **183**

KENT STATE **-9**

INDIVIDUAL LEADERS

PASSING	C/ATT	YDS	TD	INT
UA AJ McCarron	14/23	226	1	2
KS Spencer Keith	20/47	99	1	1

RUSHING	ATT	YDS	AVG	TD
UA Jalston Fowler	4	69	17.2	1
KS Jacquise Terry	10	23	2.3	0

RECEIVING	REC	YDS	LONG	TD
UA Marquis Maze	8	118	26	1
KS J. Thompson	4	19	7	1

Alabama Coach Nick Saban leads his team to the field before the Arkansas game. **PHOTO/MARK ALMOND**

Q&A WITH THE COACH

By **TOMMY HICKS**

As Alabama closed in on its second national championship in three years, columnist Tommy Hicks sat down with the architect of the Tide's success and asked head coach Nick Saban about what made the 2011 team special and what life is like as head coach of the Alabama Crimson Tide.

Q: What stands out most about this season?

SABAN: The thing I really love about this team is we have really good team chemistry, team leadership. Guys sort of bought in to doing things a certain way – made some goals and had some aspirations and really worked hard to accomplish those. Of course, we had a disappointing bump in the road and they've responded pretty well even to that, so I think that's the thing that I like most about this team. Some teams have the right stuff and some teams don't, and this team has always had the right stuff. They always try to do things the right way.

Q: Is there an aspect of this team that fans may not see but you would like to see recognized?

SABAN: I think people always assume that every team has great intangibles and that's not necessarily right. Talent is talent, and everybody knows somebody who has talent or ability but they never really converted it into a productive performance for whatever reasons.

This team has been pretty good that way, and I don't think people really think that much about it. You can't assume anything and you've got to prepare your team and you always try to do it in a culture where it's like so many things are taken for granted. As a coach and a player, you can't take those things for granted, and this team has not done that. And that's been good.

Q: What do you like most about this team?

SABAN: The toughness that this team's played with – even when we didn't play well, we've always tried to be physical. I think it's probably a little more apparent on defense, because people look at defense that way. But even up front on the offensive line, and even though our specialists haven't always performed up to expectations, even on special teams there are a lot of great hits. I'd say the physical nature of this team has been really good.

Q: What's been the biggest surprise about this team?

SABAN: Nothing really. You kind of know early on how committed people are. This team actually ended up accomplishing more than I thought. Even though we didn't beat LSU (during the regular season), I thought we did enough good things. We didn't play smart enough to win the game and we made too many penalties, errors cost us field position, negative plays in critical times. I feel bad about that myself, because as a coach I'm always sort of, "What could I have done better to prevent that from happening so we wouldn't have had those errors and we wouldn't have made those mistakes?"

Q: What's the toughest part of this job based on fan interest and going through the day-to-day duties?

SABAN: I don't know if I'm different from everybody else, but there's really only two things to me that are really, really important – recruiting good players in the program and developing those players once they get here. When I say developing players, I'm not just talking about as players. If they're going to have the kind of character and attitude they're going to need to succeed in football here, they're going to have the right kind of character to succeed in life.

Q: Do you miss not having a so-called normal existence because of your job? How tough is that part of this job?

SABAN: First of all, I never forget that you're fortunate to have the opportunity that you have. I understand what goes with that. I appreciate the opportunity that I have here, I appreciate the opportunity that I'm in and I try to do the best job that I can in that position in every way that I can do it. I appreciate all the people who support the program and have pride in it and I want to do a good job to please them to some degree, too. I never really think of those things as a negative. My dad said once, "You only have a problem if they're not asking (for autographs)." You have to keep it in perspective. But we've also always had a place where our family could go, and that's the reason for it. When you go to that place you sort of escape all that goes with this for the moment – for that weekend or couple of weeks in the summer or whatever it is. That's really good mental health and it's good for your family. We've always tried to create some balance by doing that and not get upset by doing what we have to do.

ASSISTANT COACHES

JEFF STOUTLAND

ASSISTANT HEAD COACH/OFFENSIVE LINE
Completing his first year at UA, Stoutland was previously the offensive line coach at Miami and interim head coach for the Hurricanes in the 2010 Sun Bowl. He has spent 14 years as an assistant coach at Miami, Michigan State and Syracuse. A graduate of Southern Connecticut State, Stoutland was a three-year starter at inside linebacker.

SAL SUNSERI

ASSISTANT HEAD COACH/LINEBACKERS
Sunseri, a former All-American linebacker at Pittsburgh, joined the Tide staff in 2009. He had been the defensive line coach for the NFL's Carolina Panthers since 2002. Prior to the Panthers, Sunseri coached at Michigan State, LSU, Alabama A&M, Louisville, Illinois State, Iowa Wesleyan and Pittsburgh. His son, Vinnie, is a defensive back at Alabama and son, Santino, is a quarterback at Pittsburgh.

BURTON BURNS

ASSOCIATE HEAD COACH/RUNNING BACKS
In five years with the Crimson Tide, Burns has coached two Heisman Trophy finalists, including 2009 recipient Mark Ingram and 2011 finalist Trent Richardson. He was the Football Scoop Running Backs Coach of the Year in 2008. Burns coached at Tulane and Clemson before coming to UA. He is a graduate of Nebraska, where he played fullback.

JIM McELWAIN

OFFENSIVE COORDINATOR/QUARTERBACKS
Since coming to UA in 2008, McElwain has directed the three top producing offensive units in total yardage in school history. McElwain came to the Capstone from Fresno State. Before that, he had stints with the NFL's Oakland Raiders where he coached quarterbacks, as well as Michigan State, Louisville, Montana State and Eastern Washington. He is a graduate of Eastern Washington, where he played quarterback.

BOBBY WILLIAMS

TIGHT ENDS/SPECIAL TEAMS
Williams joined the Crimson Tide staff in 2008, marking his fourth time to work on Nick Saban's coaching staff. The two previously worked together at Michigan State, LSU and with the Miami Dolphins. The Purdue graduate also spent time with the NFL's Detroit Lions, Eastern Michigan and Ball State. Williams' son, Nicholas, is a wide receiver for the Crimson Tide.

DEFENSIVE COORDINATOR/LINEBACKERS
A former standout defensive back and scholar-athlete at Georgia, Smart has been with the Tide for five seasons. After the 2009 National Championship season, Smart took home the Broyles Award as the top assistant coach in the nation. Smart came to UA after serving as safeties coach for the NFL's Miami Dolphins. Before that, he had stints at Georgia, LSU, Florida State and Valdosta State.

KIRBY SMART

DEFENSIVE LINE
In his first season with the Tide, Rumph has coached a defensive line that is ranked No.1 in rushing defense. Before coming to UA, he spent five years as defensive ends coach at Clemson. A four-year letterman and graduate of South Carolina, Rumph spent five years as head coach at Calhoun County High School (SC), then coached at South Carolina State and Memphis.

CHRIS RUMPH

DIRECTOR OF STRENGTH AND CONDITIONING
Cochran has been on Nick Saban's staff for two national titles – UA in 2009 and LSU in 2003. He was named the 2008 Samson Strength and Conditioning Coach of the Year as featured in American Football Quarterly. Prior to coming to Tuscaloosa, Cochran spent three years with the NBA's New Orleans Hornets. He has bachelor's and master's degrees from LSU.

SCOTT COCHRAN

SECONDARY
A former Crimson Tide defensive back, Pruitt joined the coaching staff in 2010 after serving as the university's director of player development. He was a student assistant coach at UA in 1997 season, then went on to coach at Plainview High School and the University of West Alabama. He also spent three seasons as defensive backs coach and defensive coordinator at Hoover High School. He is a graduate of West Alabama.

JEREMY PRUITT

RECEIVERS/RECRUITING COORDINATOR
Groh, an offensive graduate assistant at UA for the National Championship season in 2009, came back to Tuscaloosa in February 2011 after coaching quarterbacks at Louisville last year. A star quarterback at the University of Virginia, Groh spent eight seasons coaching at his alma mater. He first coached wide receivers, then added quarterbacks and also became recruiting coordinator in 2005.

MIKE GROH

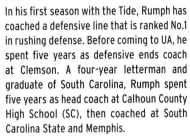

TIDE 27 NITTANY LIONS 11

Alabama defensive back DeQuan Menzie recovers a fumble by Penn State tight end Andrew Szczerba in the second quarter.

PHOTO/MARK ALMOND

Alabama defensive back Dre Kirkpatrick forces a fumble after a catch by Penn State tight end Andrew Szczerba.

PHOTO/ROBIN CONN

GRADING THE TIDE

OFFENSE

A

Five turnovers last week. None this time. The points and yards (359) are secondary.

DEFENSE

A

One forced turnover, including no fumbles forced last week. Three this week. Points and yards (251) are secondary.

SPECIAL TEAMS

A

Punting must improve, but a 44-yard punt return by Marquis Maze and a first down on a fake punt were highlights.

COACHING

A

On its opening drive, Penn State surprised Alabama with some new looks. The Tide adjusted well. The fake punt call was a bold move.

OVERALL

A

This was a quality opponent. This was a hostile environment. This was impressively methodical.

Assessment by Don Kausler, Jr.

DEFENSE PENS UP PENN STATE

By **IZZY GOULD**

STATE COLLEGE, Pa. — The energy inside Beaver Stadium ignited Penn State like the pair of jets that rattled this historic venue with a pregame flyover.

The 23rd-ranked Nittany Lions began pounding away at No. 3 Alabama surrounded by whiteout conditions – most of the 107,846 fans dressed in white shirts, with a splash of crimson in the north end zone.

The opening, 16-play drive gobbled up half of the first quarter, but Penn State could dig up only three points. That woke up Alabama's defense.

The Tide's offense got its motivational slap in the face when Alabama converted a fake punt. That unit was led by a stone-cold quarterback who proved worthy of retaining the starting job.

Alabama rolled out of Happy Valley with a 27-11 win against Penn State, taking its third straight from the Nittany Lions.

"We wanted to be aggressive today," Alabama coach Nick Saban said. "We wanted to attack."

Defensively, Alabama continued to validate the preseason buzz of potentially becoming one of program's top defenses ever. After two games, there's nothing to scoff at.

The Tide forced Penn State (1-1) to punt on its next three drives while it tried to find a pulse with quarterbacks Rob Bolden and Matt McGloin.

Alabama (2-0) charged up the offense on its second drive, the key decision coming on fourth-and-1 on the Tide's 40-yard line. Alabama lined up for a punt, but H-back Brad Smelley took the snap and managed to eke out 1 yard to keep the drive alive.

"I thought we could change the momentum of the game," Saban said. "If you're gonna take chances, sometimes you have to take them early in the game. I had a lot of confidence in our defense."

The drive continued into Penn State territory with a huge third-down conversion, a pass from quarterback AJ McCarron to wide receiver Marquis Maze. It went for 29 yards and put the Tide on Penn State's

26. Four plays later, McCarron showed his mettle by firing a pass through seemingly impossible traffic to find tight end Michael Williams for a touchdown and a 7-3 first-quarter lead.

"You can't be scared playing quarterback," McCarron said. "If you're scared, you're gonna turn the ball over. That's not how I play."

Turnovers were a concern for Alabama entering the game after it committed five in its opener. The only turnovers Saturday were those committed by the Nittany Lions – two fumbles and an interception.

The Tide played flawlessly in that regard while the defense held Penn State to 251 yards of total offense.

After taking a 10-3 lead thanks to a 22-yard field

"We wanted to be aggressive today. We wanted to attack."

Coach Nick Saban

goal in the second quarter by Jeremy Shelley, Alabama's defense produced another significant engine stopper.

Bolden connected with tight end Andrew Szczerba, who was hit by Tide defensive back Dre Kirkpatrick, dislodging the football. Cornerback DeQuan Menzie recovered it at the 50-yard line.

"It was just a good play," Kirkpatrick said. "I wasn't trying to strip it out, I was just trying to get the man on the ground."

Alabama in turn ate up all but 30 seconds before halftime by using a 10-play, 50-yard drive capped with running back Trent Richardson's 3-yard touchdown run for a 17-3 lead.

Richardson led all rushers with 26 carries for 111 yards and two touchdowns, his second giving Alabama a 27-3 lead with 6:14 to play.

"I feel like I got it going," Richardson said.

AP TOP 10	1	2	3	4	5	6	7	8	9	10
09.11.11	OKLAHOMA	ALABAMA	LSU	BOISE ST.	FLORIDA ST.	STANFORD	WISCONSIN	OK. ST.	TEXAS A&M	SO. CAROLINA

TWO STORIED PROGRAMS MILES APART

By **MIKE HERNDON**

STATE COLLEGE, Pa. — As Friday night approached Saturday morning in rain-soaked central Pennsylvania, a student with a glow stick around his neck climbed atop a makeshift platform outside Beaver Stadium.

Behind him were rows of tents. In front of him was a semi-circle of his fellow students, many of whom had camped in what's known as Paternoville since Monday in order to get front-row seats in the student section for Saturday's Alabama game.

They beat on plastic garbage cans and sang crude songs about Ohio State and Pitt, but they tolerated no abuse of the week's opponent, shouting down a classmate who dared boo the Crimson Tide.

"They took care of us down there," the boy on the platform yelled. "We need to treat them well up here."

The heyday of this rivalry was before these kids were born, but they understand it just the same. This is Joe Paterno, Bear Bryant and, now, Nick Saban. It's Barry Krauss and Shane Conlan, Bobby Humphrey and Matt Suhey. This is what college football is all about.

These are two of only eight FBS programs that have won more than 800 games, and their respect for each other seems to trickle down to the most obnoxious fan. But Saturday's game showed they are in much different places right now.

Penn State hopes to contend in the Big Ten. Alabama expects to contend for the national title.

Penn State hoped to catch Alabama off-guard with off-balance formations and misdirection runs. Alabama expected to be tested and to adjust.

Penn State hoped for one of its quarterbacks to step forward. Alabama expected Mobile's AJ McCarron to take control and lead the team.

Penn State hoped to contain Trent Richardson. Alabama expected its defense to dominate.

The Crimson Tide met practically all of those expectations Saturday. McCarron looked comfortable and poised in throwing for 163 yards, a touchdown and no interceptions.

He waited a long time for this day. When it finally came in front of a white-out crowd of 107,846 – the largest crowd ever to see an Alabama game – he expected to walk out of Beaver Stadium with a win.

"I've been playing football since I was 4," he said afterward. "It's just another day."

The Crimson Tide knew it was better than Penn State, then went out and proved it, passing the first test toward meeting the ultimate expectation – a national title.

(Right) Alabama running back Eddie Lacy eyes Penn State cornerback Chaz Powell in the fourth quarter. PHOTO/MARK ALMOND

Alabama quarterback AJ McCarron looks to throw behind the blocking of offensive lineman Anthony Steen.

PHOTO/MARK ALMOND

Alabama defensive backs Vinnie Sunseri and Will Lowery celebrate with Alabama defensive back Dre Kirkpatrick after Kirkpatrick caused a Penn State fumble that was recovered by Alabama in the fourth quarter.

PHOTO/ MARK ALMOND

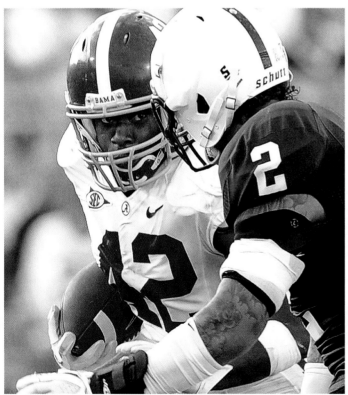

	1	2	3	4	FINAL
ALABAMA	7	10	3	7	27
PENN STATE	3	0	0	8	11

TOTAL YARDS

ALABAMA **359**

PENN STATE **251**

PASSING YARDS

ALABAMA **163**

PENN STATE **144**

RUSHING YARDS

ALABAMA **196**

PENN STATE **107**

INDIVIDUAL LEADERS

PASSING	C/ATT	YDS	TD	INT
UA AJ McCarron	19/31	163	1	0
PS Rob Bolden	11/29	144	0	1
RUSHING	ATT	YDS	AVG	TD
UA Trent Richardson	26	111	4.3	2
PS Silas Redd	22	65	3.0	1
RECEIVING	REC	YDS	LONG	TD
UA Marquis Maze	4	42	29	0
PS Derek Moye	3	51	27	0

By DON KAUSLER, JR.

TUSCALOOSA — The ball changes hands, a series is about to start, and the flurry before the fury begins.

An opposing offense huddles on the far sideline, and on the field stand 15 members of Alabama's defense.

Quarterbacks might think they're playing against 15 defenders sometimes when they face a Nick Saban defense, but for now this is no mirage. There really are four more than 11 Alabama players standing there with their eyes focused on their own sideline.

The offense breaks its huddle, and in the coaches' box, two or three blinks result in one read and reaction. One word is communicated to the coaches on the sidelines.

"Red!"

Red? All of the offensive personnel groups are color-coded, Saban explained.

"If we yell out red, there's four wideouts in the game," he said.

A student assistant holds up a sign that spells out the color with red letters.

"All of our guys know what we're going to play against red," Saban said.

But it doesn't stop with a shout or a sign. Defensive coordinator Kirby Smart is the maestro, orchestrating this movement. He holds two hands up. Each hand flashes five fingers.

Dime defense is the call.

Inside linebacker Nico Johnson comes off the field. Inside linebacker C.J. Mosley stays. Run-stopping nose guard Josh Chapman runs off. Pass-rushing defensive lineman Nick Gentry stays. Defensive end Jesse Williams and strong outside linebacker Jerrell Harris sprint to the sideline. Cornerback Dee Milliner and safety Will Lowery stay. Middle linebacker Dont'a Hightower moves to de-

fensive end. Cornerback DeQuan Menzie moves to "star," Saban's name for nickel back.

Before the quarterback is lining up in the shotgun, everyone's in position. The quarterback checks from a pass to a draw play, and a running back trying to get outside is stopped for a 1-yard loss.

Welcome to the world of situational defense.

Saban didn't invent it, but he has perfected it, and he is passionate when he talks about his craft, about how offenses adopt and defenses adapt.

In a recent one-on-one interview, one wizard allowed a peek behind his curtain.

EVOLUTION AND EVALUATION

Fifty years ago, linemen often still played both offense and defense. Backs carried the ball and covered receivers.

Twenty-five years ago, defense still was far from what it is.

As the defensive coordinator at Michigan State as late as 1987, Saban said he seldom used a nickel defense. "We played everything with regular people," he said.

The next year, he was introduced to the NFL as a Houston Oilers assistant coach.

"That was the first time I started to see that you've got to match up the personnel," Saban said. "The skill guys can't get covered by the linebackers."

Run-and-shoot offenses and other spreads were revolutionizing football.

"Then when I went back to be the head coach at Toledo, we played nickel," Saban said. That was 1990. "We just matched up the personnel. But in those days, I tried to do both. We tried to adjust regular against it, and now here's nickel. What happened was, you don't have time to practice all this stuff. You can't take the same play that they run with three wideouts and rep it with regular people, and then rep it with nickel or dime people."

He returned to the NFL in 1991 and coached four seasons with the Cleveland Browns.

"It was 100 percent specialized," Saban said of pro defenses.

In 1995, Saban returned to Michigan State as the head coach.

"Everybody said, 'Well, you really can't do that in college,'" he said of substituting according to offensive personnel. "And I said, 'Well, you can't do it the other way, because you don't have time to practice everything.' That's how it's evolved into what it is now.

"It was cause and effect for me. It wasn't like a new invention."

Alabama linebacker C.J. Mosley flattens Kent State wide receiver Sam Kirkland in the third quarter at Bryant-Denny Stadium.   PHOTO/MARK ALMOND

Offensive changes continued to spread.

"All of a sudden we have to have a bigger package, because nickel used to be just for pass defense," Saban said. "Now we've got to stop the runs out of it, so that started to grow.

"Now it's gone even further. You specialize not only in matching the personnel, but now the situations within that, in terms of third-down, two-minute, red area, maybe when they get close to the goal line you play something else. Then you have a couple of different rush groups that may strictly be the best players you have to go execute something."

Alabama linebacker Jerrell Harris (left) and defensive lineman Ed Stinson sandwich Arkansas quarterback Tyler Wilson in the first quarter. PHOTO/MARK ALMOND

LSU quarterback Jordan Jefferson is brought sacked behind the line of scrimmage by Alabama defensive lineman Damion Square and Alabama linebacker C.J. Mosley.   PHOTO/BILL STARLING

TIDE 41 MEAN GREEN 0

TIDE MEANER THAN GREEN

By **IZZY GOULD**

TUSCALOOSA — Alabama's 41-0 disposal of an overmatched North Texas team signaled the end of the tinkering and tune-ups for the second-ranked Crimson Tide.

Ready or not, it's time for Alabama to test itself against some SEC competition beginning with No. 14 Arkansas at Bryant-Denny Stadium.

The late-round knockout of North Texas came courtesy of running backs Trent Richardson and Eddie Lacy while the defense pitched its first shutout since a 45-0 win against Chattanooga in 2009.

Richardson and Lacy both had career games while the offense amassed 586 yards. They were the first pair of Alabama running backs to go for at least 150 yards and touchdowns in a single game.

Richardson's night was worthy of stirring up more Heisman Trophy candidacy conversation. He put up a career-high 167 yards rushing on 11 carries, highlighted by his 71-yard, fourth-quarter touchdown. Richardson also matched his career high with three touchdowns, giving him eight touchdowns in three games.

Just after Richardson appeared to be breaking away with the night's accolades, Lacy broke of the longest run of his career – a 67-yarder to put

TRAGEDY TO TRIUMPH

Alabama's DeAndrew White tackles North Texas' Brelon Chancellor on a kickoff return in the fourth quarter.

PHOTO/MIKE KITTRELL

Alabama ahead 41-0 in the fourth quarter.

Lacy finished with nine carries for a career-high 161 yards while matching his career best with two TDs.

"They did a great job, got to the second level and it was off to the races," center William Vlachos said. "We expect that type of stuff from them."

The running game was about the only thing that could overshadow Alabama's defense, which limited North Texas to 169 yards of total offense.

The Mean Green was held to one first down in the first half and did not cross into Alabama territory until the second half.

Probably the toughest task for the defense came in the fourth quarter when North Texas had two sets of downs at the Alabama 2.

Playing with reserves at that point, coach Nick Saban quipped about angling to preserve the shutout.

"That was some real coaching going on there, man," he said. "There was a lot of second- and third-team guys in there. Not only held them once, but held them twice. You've got to like the way the players competed."

The Tide defense was led by safeties Mark Barron and Will Lowery, each with seven tackles.

Offensively, Alabama used quarterbacks AJ McCarron and Phillip Sims. McCarron, who has started all three games, appeared to cement his place as the No. 1 quarterback by completing 15-of-21 passes for 190 yards. Sims, who played in only the final two minutes at Penn State, looked more comfortable in his second game.

"It was obviously a good win," Saban said. "The goal of what we were trying to do was improve as a team."

GRADING THE TIDE

OFFENSE

B

Alabama piled up yards (586) but didn't always dominate, and lost two fumbles. The Tide can't afford that against Arkansas.

DEFENSE

A

The Tide forced no turnovers, but it pitched a shutout.

SPECIAL TEAMS

B

Jeremy Shelley made only 2 of 4 field goals. Marquis Maze had a 28-yard punt return. The Tide contained North Texas star kick returner Brelon Chancellor.

COACHING

A

The mix of plays for starters and backups seemed just right.

OVERALL

B

The Tide was just a little sloppy against a team it shoud have plastered.

Assessment by Don Kausler, Jr.

Alabama running back Trent Richardson leaves the North Texas defensive unit in his `wake on the way to a 71-yard touchdown in the fourth quarter.

PHOTO/MARK ALMOND

CRIMSON TIDE IS STILL A MYSTERY

By **DOUG SEGREST**

North Texas defensive back D'Leon McCord catches Alabama running back Eddie Lacy but not before he scores a 43-yard touchdown in the second quarter.

PHOTO/MARK ALMOND

	1	2	3	4	FINAL
ALABAMA	10	10	7	14	41
NO. TEXAS	0	0	0	0	0

TOTAL YARDS
ALABAMA **586**
NO. TEXAS **169**

PASSING YARDS
ALABAMA **239**
NO. TEXAS **101**

RUSHING YARDS
ALABAMA **347**
NO. TEXAS **68**

INDIVIDUAL LEADERS

PASSING	C/ATT	YDS	TD	INT
UA AJ McCarron	15/21	190	0	0
NT Derek Thompson	11/22	80	0	0

RUSHING	ATT	YDS	AVG	TD
UA Trent Richardson	11	167	15.2	3
NT James Hamilton	7	33	4.7	0

RECEIVING	REC	YDS	LONG	TD
UA Kenny Bell	4	55	25	0
NT Lance Dunbar	4	45	20	0

TUSCALOOSA — Go ahead, deny it if you can. You've had Nov. 5 circled since LSU made a statement about football fashion and old-school defense two weeks ago against Oregon.

The road to Atlanta, the road to New Orleans, the road to the SEC's sixth straight BCS title goes through Bryant-Denny Stadium that day. LSU comes to Alabama, giving college football two possible unbeatens and a potential No. 1 vs. No. 2 regular-season showdown as epic as Oklahoma-Nebraska 40 years ago.

Uh, hold that thought.

The road to paradise may indeed go through Tuscaloosa, but don't look down the road. Look dead ahead.

Look at CBS' lineup: Arkansas at Alabama this Saturday afternoon.

The Razorbacks may not be the Razorbacks of old. The difference? They play respectable defense now. Combine that with a lethal passing attack that will challenge what many fans and media consider the nation's premier secondary, and you have the makings of Game of the Century, the prequel.

Arkansas has an identity, on both sides of the ball, even if the competition hasn't been sterling. As for Alabama, to quote Winston Churchill, the second-ranked Crimson Tide is "a riddle, wrapped in a mystery, inside an enigma."

Truth is, even after a no-frills 3-0 start, we don't know much about Nick Saban's 2011 work in progress.

The defense is very good. But even in pitching a 41-0 shutout Saturday, Alabama only proved again that it can manhandle anemic offenses. Penn State is a Big Ten member but has not yet shown an offensive pulse.

The Tide offense remains vanilla. At least the quarterback controversy is over. AJ McCarron proved that a little experience goes a long way against North Texas. Phillip Sims may be his equal in terms of arm strength, but an offense that was humming under McCarron lost momentum when Sims came in.

Sims wasn't the only newcomer Saturday. Tide coaches traded out tackles and tailbacks. The consistency wasn't the same with the second group.

Tide coaches have a better feel for how McCarron will handle adversity. He has won in a hostile environment. He is the clear-cut starter.

But that's about all we know.

Alabama gashed a North Texas defense that ranks among the worst in the nation with long touchdown runs. The Tide averaged better than 10 yards a pop, a nod more to its explosiveness than its ability to pound.

Alabama was methodical against North Texas. That's the Tide's personality. Think of the guy you knew in college who hunkered down in the library, avoided parties and turned out to be the CEO of a Fortune 500 company.

> ## "It's just you and the touchdown. It's one of the greatest feelings ever."
>
> *Running back Eddie Lacy on his 67-yard touchdown run during which he checked himself out on the stadium's video screen to make sure no defenders were catching him*

AP TOP 10	1	2	3	4	5	6	7	8	9	10
09.18.11	OKLAHOMA	LSU	ALABAMA	BOISE ST.	STANFORD	WISCONSIN	OK. ST.	TEXAS A&M	NEBRASKA	OREGON

67

TIDE (38) RAZORBACKS (14)

Alabama running back Trent Richardson looks to outrun Arkansas cornerback Darius Winston (21) as Richardson gains yardage to set up a TD.

PHOTO/GLENN BAESKE

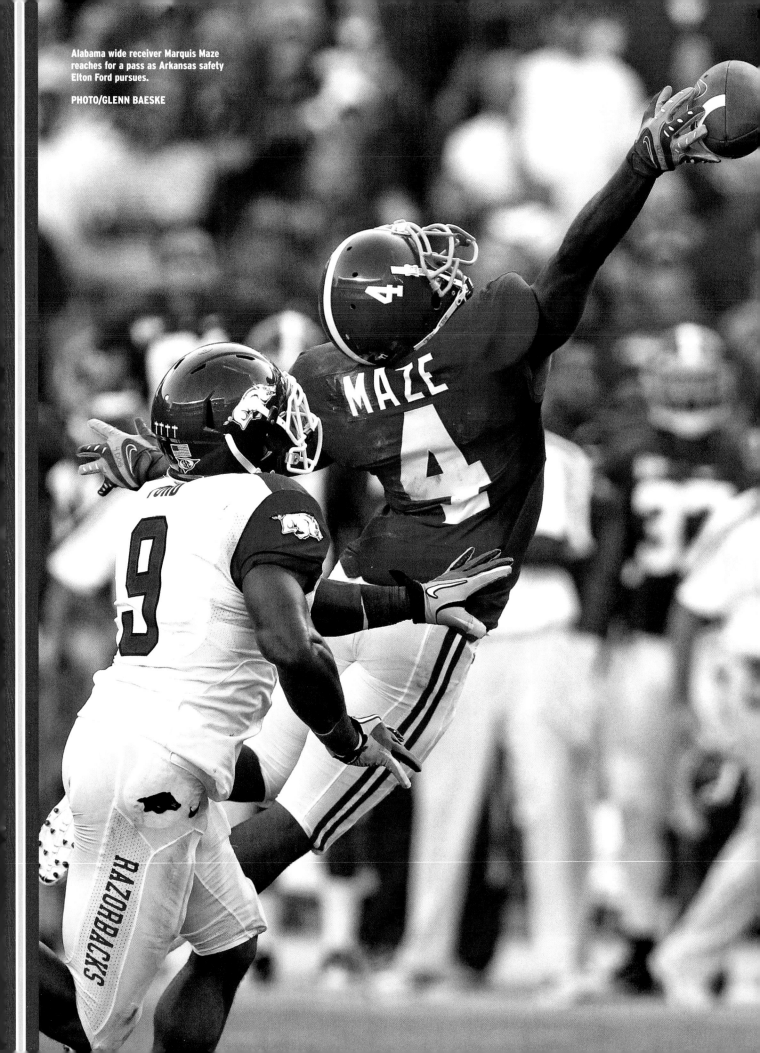

Alabama wide receiver Marquis Maze reaches for a pass as Arkansas safety Elton Ford pursues.

PHOTO/GLENN BAESKE

GRADING THE TIDE

OFFENSE

B

The Tide averaged 5.1 yards per rush, completed 75 percent of its passes and had no turnovers. There was a big red-zone failure.

DEFENSE

A

The defense made potent Arkansas one-dimensional by taking away the run (17 yards on 19 carries).

SPECIAL TEAMS

A

Fake FG for a touchdown, an 83-yard punt return by Marquis Maze and good coverage added up to a season-best showing.

COACHING

A

Alabama coach Nick Saban lauded defensive coordinator Kirby Smart for his quick and decisive calls throughout the game.

OVERALL

A

If there was any doubt this is a national championship contender, there's no doubt now. This was a complete, impressive performance.

Assessment by Don Kausler, Jr.

BAMA OVERPOWERS HOGS

By **IZZY GOULD**

TUSCALOOSA — Microphones couldn't capture the eyes. No matter how sharp the words, the looks on the faces told more.

Alabama's players told reporters what happened Saturday, but the Tide's deeper stares told the real story.

This team has killer instinct.

Third-ranked Alabama pummeled No. 14 Arkansas with an unforgiving display of dominance in a 38-14 victory in front of 101,821 fans at Bryant-Denny Stadium.

What drove the Tide?

"They (the Razorbacks) were doing a lot of talking as well," said Alabama safety Mark Barron. "So we most definitely wanted to shut that up."

The winning began with the opening coin flip.

Alabama wanted the ball so it could swing its fist first and hard.

The bully mentality resulted in an 80-yard opening drive that ended with a touchdown pass from AJ McCarron to Michael Williams disguised initially as a 54-yard field goal attempt on fourth-and-4 at Arkansas' 37-yard line.

Arkansas (3-1, 0-1) offered its best counter punch in the first quarter with a power drive of its own. Quarterback Tyler Wilson (22-for-35, 185 yards, two touchdowns, one interception) completed a 63-yard drive to tie the game at 7 after a 10-yard touchdown pass to Dennis Johnson.

Alabama went on a roll for the next four scores to take a 31-7 lead through three quarters.

It began with an interception by Alabama defensive back DeQuan Menzie, who tipped a Wilson pass in the air, then made a basket catch and raced 25 yards for a touchdown.

Menzie's play was one highlight of the defense, which held Arkansas to 226 yards of offense, including a mere 17 rushing.

The Tide was led by linebacker Dont'a Hightower's nine tackles, and strong secondary play from Dre Kirkpatrick (six tackles, three pass breakups) and Mark Barron (six tackles, one pass breakup).

"It was a little personal, but I had to adjust to what they were doing," Kirkpatrick said. "I knew they were gonna go out and try to throw some different things at me. Mark Barron being one of the great leaders out there kept me calm, kept me focused. Last year I think I got too emotional."

Menzie's play was outdone by probably the play of the year to this point, an 83-yard punt return for a touchdown by Tide senior Marquis Maze.

Maze dazzled the crowd with quick thinking and patience as he unzipped the coverage and waited for his blockers to set up the final wall.

"Once I beat the punter, some guy had an angle on me so I just waited on the block," Maze said. "I saw

"I don't think this is our best day."

Wide receiver Marquis Maze when asked about the Tide's potential following a dominating win over Arkansas

my guys running down. Once they made the block, I cut back, and then it was just me running."

Running back Trent Richardson turned the game into a rout when he took a screen pass from McCarron then raced 61 yards for a touchdown. He finished with a game-high 17 carries for 126 yards rushing and 235 all-purpose yards.

Perhaps the only blemish was an Arkansas goal-line stand in the second quarter when Arkansas stuffed three straight rushing attempts from its 1-yard line, forcing the Tide to settle for a Jeremy Shelley field goal.

Richardson said Alabama later made adjustments, which allowed Eddie Lacy to pound in the final touchdown from 4 yards out in the third quarter.

"They did a lot of stuff we weren't prepared for," Richardson said. "They came off the back side pretty hard. And we just had to adjust to it. We were ready to get back on the goal line again."

And quiet the Razorbacks one more time.

AP TOP 10	1	2	3	4	5	6	7	8	9	10
09.25.11	LSU	OKLAHOMA	ALABAMA	BOISE ST.	OK. ST.	STANFORD	WISCONSIN	NEBRASKA	OREGON	SO. CAROLINA

NO DRAMA WITH TIDE DEFENDERS

By **RANDY KENNEDY**

TUSCALOOSA — How can a game that featured a 37-yard touchdown on a trick play, a pick-six by the defense and an amazing punt return that officially covered 83 yards have no real drama?

The answer: When the Alabama defense is on the field. It is suffocating (yielding 17 net yards on 19 carries Saturday), opportunistic (two interceptions, including DeQuan Menzie's 25-yard TD return) and intimidating (for a second straight game, the opposing coach chose to pull his starting quarterback to spare him any additional abuse).

But it is not big on suspense.

For the fourth time in four games, Alabama scored all the points it needed in the first half Saturday. The Crimson Tide and Arkansas could

Alabama running back Eddie Lacy drags Arkansas linebacker Matt Marshall for a 4-yard touchdown in the fourth quarter. **PHOTO/MARK ALMOND**

still be playing at this minute and the Razorbacks still wouldn't have matched the 38 points Alabama scored.

"It was a great team win," said coach Nick Saban, who dutifully pointed out areas in which his team can improve but didn't try to suppress his satisfaction with the performance.

The Crimson Tide has been so dominant that after beating No. 14 Arkansas 38-14, it saw its scoring average go down and its points allowed per game go up. And the defense stifled the Razorbacks without any special tricks.

"We only really blitzed one time today and that's when they hit us for their second touchdown," Saban said.

As good as the defense has been, it's easy to overlook how far sophomore quarterback AJ McCarron has come. He is now one of the SEC's most efficient passers and the clear leader of the Alabama offense. (Note to the Bryant-Denny game-day staff: It's time to stop including McCarron and Phillip Sims on the big screen as the starting quarterback during pregame introductions.)

McCarron completed 75 percent of his passes against Arkansas and directed an offense that put up 200 yards passing and 197 rushing. For the third straight game, he did not turn the ball over. On Saturday, the coaches showed their confidence in him by starting in a no-huddle attack.

The Crimson Tide must visit Florida next, but this team has a different feel than last year's three-loss team. The No. 1 difference is perhaps attitude.

"I don't think this is our best day," said Marquis Maze, who scored on the 83-yard punt return Saturday.

That day will be exciting for Alabama fans, but probably not very suspenseful.

Alabama tight end Michael Williams celebrates with Alabama kicker Cade Foster after scoring a touchdown on a fake field goal attempt in the first quarter. **PHOTO/MARK ALMOND**

Alabama defensive back DeQuan Menzie returns an interception for a touchdown in the second quarter.

PHOTO/MARK ALMOND

	1	2	3	4	FINAL
ALABAMA	7	10	21	0	38
ARKANSAS	7	0	7	0	14

TOTAL YARDS
ALABAMA **397**
ARKANSAS **226**

PASSING YARDS
ALABAMA **200**
ARKANSAS **209**

RUSHING YARDS
ALABAMA **197**
ARKANSAS **17**

INDIVIDUAL LEADERS

PASSING	C/ATT	YDS	TD	INT
UA AJ McCarron	15/20	200	2	0
AR Tyler Wilson	22/35	185	2	1

RUSHING	ATT	YDS	AVG	TD
UA Trent Richardson	17	126	7.4	0
AR R. Wingo Jr.	11	35	3.2	0

RECEIVING	REC	YDS	LONG	TD
UA Marquis Maze	5	40	17	0
AR Joe Adams	6	37	19	0

TIDE 38   GATORS 10

Alabama defensive back Mark Barron (left) and Alabama linebacker Dont'a Hightower (middle) combine to stop Florida running back Chris Rainey in the first quarter.

PHOTO/G.M. ANDREWS

Alabama running back Trent Richardson dives for extra yardage in the second quarter.

PHOTO/MARK ALMOND

GRADING THE TIDE

OFFENSE

B

Playing with a mission, Florida native Trent Richardson piled up 208 all-purpose yards.

DEFENSE

A

Courtney Upshaw came up with an interception return for a TD and knocked out Florida QB John Brantley.

SPECIAL TEAMS

B

The highlight was a 70-yard kickoff return by Marquis Maze to set up the Tide's first touchdown.

COACHING

A

A solid plan was well executed, and the staff helped the Tide keep its poise when it trailed early.

OVERALL

A

A four-touchdown victory on the road against another ranked team. How can anyone not be impressed?

Assessment by Don Kausler, Jr.

STOMPIN' THROUGH THE SWAMP

By **IZZY GOULD**

GAINESVILLE, Fla — History suggests Florida has become one of the toughest places to win a football game.

The 90,888 fans who stuffed themselves inside Ben Hill Griffin Stadium on Saturday night – the second-largest crowd in school history – only added to the legend of Florida Field.

And when John Brantley launched a deep pass on Florida's first offensive play, Andre Debose raced past Dre Kirkpatrick, snatching it and sprinting away for a 65-yard touchdown.

The Swamp was suddenly Animal House, a tangled celebration of orange and blue.

How would Alabama respond?

With the backbone of a winner.

"The goal tonight was to attack and be aggressive from the very start," Alabama coach Nick Saban said. "At the beginning we were maybe too hyped up. It really shows the resiliency of our team."

The third-ranked Crimson Tide defeated No. 12 Florida 38-10. Alabama (5-0, 2-0) scored 35 unanswered points while Florida (4-1, 2-1) watched helplessly.

The Gators could not stop junior running back Trent Richardson. The Pensacola native rushed for a career-high 29 carries and 181 yards, including two touchdowns.

It was Alabama's first win at Florida since 1999 when the Tide rallied for a 40-39 overtime victory.

A kaleidoscope of runs, hits and dynamite destroyed the kitchen sink that Florida offensive coordinator Charlie Weis promised to throw at the Tide.

Richardson was aided by solid run blocking and complemented by the poised pocket presence of AJ McCarron (12-for-25 passing, 140 yards).

It was a lightning-quick lick from linebacker Courtney Upshaw in the second quarter that helped the Tide begin to take control for good.

With the game tied at 10, Upshaw gobbled up Florida speedster Chris Rainey for a 7-yard loss. Then Upshaw intercepted Brantley two plays later and sprinted 45 yards untouched for a momentum-changing touchdown. It was the second pick-six in as many games for Alabama, and the second year in a row the Tide returned an interception against Florida for a score.

Upshaw led Alabama with four tackles, including three for losses, and a sack.

The Gators' offense, which relied heavily on its passing game, was suddenly silenced.

> ## "That's what we do as a defense: punish people and hit them."
>
> *Linebacker Courtney Upshaw after knocking Florida quarterback John Brantley out of the game*

And it would get worse for the Gators.

Upshaw sacked Florida's starting quarterback two plays before halftime, knocking him out of the game.

Alabama's defense was stifling, holding Florida to 222 total yards, including three sacks, four fumbles (one lost) and an interception.

The Tide smothered the Gators' normally effective running game of Rainey and Jeff Demps, who rushed a combined 14 times for 8 yards. Florida had just 15 rushing yards for the game.

"We got beat by a better team tonight," Florida coach Will Muschamp said.

AP TOP 10	1	2	3	4	5	6	7	8	9	10
10.02.11	LSU	ALABAMA	OKLAHOMA	WISCONSIN	BOISE ST.	OK. ST.	STANFORD	CLEMSON	OREGON	ARKANSAS

ALABAMA SILENCES, THEN EMPTIES SWAMP

Florida quarterback John Brantley grimaces in pain as he is sacked by Alabama linebacker Courtney Upshaw in the second quarter.

PHOTO/G.M. ANDREWS

By **KEVIN SCARBINSKY**

GAINESVILLE, Fla. — How loud was the Swamp at the start Saturday night?

It was so loud, Nick Saban couldn't hear himself scream.

Will Muschamp, either.

And nobody screams like the head coaches at Alabama and Florida. It's another lesson the student learned from the teacher.

Saban no doubt raised his voice a decibel or two after the home team's first snap as Andre Debose ran away from Dre Kirkpatrick for a 65-yard touchdown pass.

That lightning strike was followed by some serious thunder. The second-largest crowd in stadium history, 90,888 strong, became the loudest gathering ever in this house at that moment.

It was a flashback to the last time a new Florida coach met Alabama in the flesh for the first time, in reverse. On a sunny day in Tuscaloosa in 2005, Brodie Croyle and Tyrone Prothro combined for a long, quick touchdown strike for the Crimson Tide, right in Urban Meyer's face, and the rout was on.

There's one big difference, though, between this Alabama team and that Florida team.

That Florida team wasn't yet a championship team.

This Alabama team is well on its way. To another SEC crown and beyond.

Hit these guys in the mouth, they hit you back.

Who's going to challenge Alabama after Florida went down 38-10, after the visitors emptied the Swamp of many of its fans and most of its bite long before the clock struck midnight?

Seriously.

At this very moment, there's zero doubt that the two best college football teams in America are Alabama and LSU. Put them in whichever order you like.

I prefer Alabama 1A and LSU 1B, but that's me. Seeing in person is believing.

The Tide and Tigers will separate themselves Nov. 5 in Tuscaloosa. Until then, there's not a worthy challenger on the horizon for the men in the red hats. That's not hyperbole. That's cold, hard fact.

Florida looked like it might make Alabama sweat, at least for an energetic moment, but it turned out that the Crimson Tide is more cold-blooded than the Gators.

It might not seem like a trophy-worthy accomplishment to beat a team with a first-year head coach that was forced to play the entire second half with a true freshman backup quarterback.

Well, sure, when you put it like that, this won't go down as a Crimson Classic.

But if you think just any college football team could've walked into this atmosphere and taken the air out of the place with a performance that was both physically imposing and emotionally paralyzing, you weren't here.

You didn't see the Alabama defense turn Florida sprinters Chris Rainey and Jeff Demps into track stars with nowhere to run, despite feeling the wind of the crowd at their backs.

The Gators scored an encouraging 10 points in the first 10 energizing minutes. And didn't score again.

If you didn't feel the earth move after Florida's opening touchdown, you can't totally appreciate the ferocity of the Alabama offense's response, primarily in the person of Trent Richardson and his escorts. They ran into the teeth of the Florida defense and extracted those teeth one by one.

Without Novocain, no less.

Richardson is the kind of football player Rainey and Demps would like to be when they grow up, even though, like most humans, they have no chance to grow to that size and maintain that speed.

After watching Richardson shake, rattle and roll for a career-high 181 yards and two touchdowns, it would be an injustice not to stop and offer the following unpaid political advertisement.

"34 Heisman."

That is all. There's nothing left to see or say. The Swamp is drained and silent.

Alabama quarterback AJ McCarron celebrates following the Crimson Tide's 38-10 win. PHOTO/G.M. ANDREWS

	1	2	3	4	FINAL
ALABAMA	10	14	0	14	38
FLORIDA	10	0	0	0	10

TOTAL YARDS

ALABAMA **366**

FLORIDA **222**

PASSING YARDS

ALABAMA **140**

FLORIDA **207**

RUSHING YARDS

ALABAMA **226**

FLORIDA **15**

INDIVIDUAL LEADERS

PASSING	C/ATT	YDS	TD	INT
UA AJ McCarron	12/25	140	0	0
UF J. Brantley	11/16	190	1	1
RUSHING	**ATT**	**YDS**	**AVG**	**TD**
UA Trent Richardson	29	181	6.2	2
UF J. Driskel	6	18	3.0	0
RECEIVING	**REC**	**YDS**	**LONG**	**TD**
UA Michael Williams	3	32	22	0
UF J. Reed	5	31	10	0

(Left) Alabama running back Trent Richardson and wide receiver Darius Hanks celebrates Richardson's fourth-quarter touchdown.

PHOTO/MARK ALMOND

Florida quarterback Jeff Driskel is stopped by Alabama linebacker Alex Watkins (91), defensive lineman Damion Square (92) and defensive lineman Josh Chapman (99) in the third quarter.

PHOTO/G.M. ANDREWS

TIDE 34   COMMODORES 0

TIDE NOT IN FULL STRIDE

By **DON KAUSLER, JR.**

TUSCALOOSA — An Alabama football team that is chasing greatness was merely very good against Vanderbilt.

The second-ranked Crimson Tide (6-0, 3-0 in the Southeastern Conference) started slowly but still was more than good enough to defeat the Commodores 34-0 on homecoming at Bryant-Denny Stadium.

You've heard of moral victories? This almost sounded like a moral defeat, because the Crimson Tide didn't dominate the Commodores

(3-2, 1-2) for all four quarters. It rallied from a mere 14-0 halftime lead.

"We played a pretty good (second) half, but as a whole game, I'm not sure we played our best game," junior left tackle Barrett Jones said, "and every time we take the field, we want to play our best game up to that point."

Alabama coach Nick Saban was not pleased.

"We didn't have the mental energy and intensity that we like to have, to play with the kind of consistency that we need to improve as a team," he said.

The Tide went three-and-out on two of its first three possessions.

"I thought we came out flat," said senior tight end Brad Smelley, who caught his first career touchdown pass in the first quarter. "Obviously we want to start faster than that."

The defense allowed Vanderbilt to drive into field-goal position twice in the first half, but the Commodores missed both kicks.

"We kind of got off to a rocky start, made a lot of mental errors in the first half," junior linebacker Nico Johnson said. "We were kind of disappointed in that."

The second half was a different story. Alabama held Vanderbilt to 48 yards in the last two quarters. For the game, the Commodores never drove inside the Tide's 20-yard line.

Alabama did plenty of things well. The defense pitched its second shutout of the season and grabbed two second-half interceptions. The offense committed no turnovers.

AJ McCarron completed 23 of 30 passes for 237 yards and a career-high four touchdowns.

Trent Richardson rushed for 107 yards, giving him five consecutive 100-yard games, and he scored his 12th touchdown of the season on a 1-yard run.

A team that had scored touchdowns at only a 55 percent rate in the red zone in its first five games went 4-for-5 in the red zone this time.

All five of Alabama's touchdowns came on third-down plays. It came into the game with a rate of 44 percent on third-down conversions but converted 12 of 17 third-down plays (71 percent).

Best of all, it put together touchdown drives of 77 yards (10 plays), 78 yards (13 plays), 94 yards (12 plays) and 81 yards (nine plays). Starting at the end of the second quarter, it scored on four consecutive possessions.

It opened the second half with a three-and-out on defense and then the 94-yard drive. Richardson ran eight times for 64 yards on the drive.

"That 95-yard drive kind of set the tone for the whole half," Jones said.

Richardson summed up the Tide's feelings about underachieving in the wake of a 38-10 victory the previous week at No. 12 Florida.

"We really just want to be relentless and have every team fear us, just don't want to play us," he said. "That's one thing we need to get better at. If we want to be that relentless team, we've got to play all four quarters like we did the second half."

Alabama tight end Brad Smelley catches a first-quarter touchdown pass in front of Vanderbilt safety Karl Butler.

PHOTO/MARK ALMOND

TIDE ROLLING ON

Pair of No. 4s, Maze and Barron, lead another rout.

By **MARK McCARTER**

TUSCALOOSA — There's a history of jersey-identity crisis at Alabama already.

Who's your No. 12? Ken Stabler? Joe Namath? Pat Trammell? Greg McElroy?

Who's your 22? Johnny Musso? Mark Ingram?

What about 73? Billy Neighbors? John Hannah? William Vlachos?

Why, if Alabama started to retire numbers of deserving players, it'd have to go to triple-digits, and the rules of football frown on that.

Usually, the jersey-identity crisis doesn't happen the same year.

It does now.

Who's your fave 4?

Marquis Maze?

Or Mark Barron?

"They're running a tight race," said linebacker Nico Johnson.

"That's a tough question. Mark Barron is a really hard hitter, and Maze is a playmaker. They're about neck-and-neck," said receiver Darius Hanks.

With such overpopulated rosters, college teams find it necessary to employ duplicate numbers. Typically, a seldom-used reserve on one side of the ball will wear the same number as a regular on the other side. John Fulton, a defensive back from Manning, S.C., wears No. 10, same as quarterback AJ McCarron, for instance.

This year at Alabama, No. 4 is worn by two stars. Both shone equally in Saturday's 34-0 avalanche over Vanderbilt that improved Alabama to 6-0. (Hey, the Tide is officially bowl eligible, in case you were worried.)

Safety Mark Barron, the senior from Mobile, led the Tide with six tackles. More than anything, he led the Tide emotionally.

Alabama was flat as a tortilla in the first half.

An understandably cranky Nick Saban complained that "we just didn't have the sense of purpose that we need, and this is the moral challenge that we all have — to overcome human nature and to get satisfied too easily."

He fussed about Alabama's lack of "mental energy and intensity that we like to have."

So did Barron.

GRADING THE TIDE

OFFENSE

B

Highlights: Four long touchdown drives and 12 of 17 on third-down conversions.

DEFENSE

A

The Tide bent a little early but then stiffened, holding Vanderbilt to 48 yards in the second half.

SPECIAL TEAMS

C

This was average. No real highs or lows, though Jeremy Shelley missed a PAT kick.

COACHING

B

The Tide was flat in the first half, and coaches are accountable, but key halftime adjustments were made.

OVERALL

B

This was not a big step forward or backward for a team with the highest standards.

Assessment by Don Kausler, Jr.

Turns out, it's not just coaches who give Gipper speeches at halftime. Barron preached one on this gorgeously moonlit Saturday evening. His teammates listened – or else.

"He was talking about this is not our D. This is not Alabama football," Johnson related. "We're better than that. He said we can't take a step from last week. We kinda took a step forward. We're kinda taking a step back (tonight). He was telling us we should have learned last year from our losses, from not finishing.

"That," Johnson said, "kind of motivated our defense."

On the other side of the ball, Maze, the senior from Birmingham, had a career-high nine receptions, for 93 yards.

Trent Richardson may be Alabama's best player, but Maze may be its most electrifying. His incredible 83-yard punt return two weeks ago against Arkansas is destined to join the other immortal video-board highlights to which Tide fans bask in pregame.

"He's elusive," Hanks said. "You can put him at running back, receiver, kick returner, punt returner, everything."

Maze didn't get a touchdown reception, though McCarron passed for four TDs. They were doled out to Hanks, Brad Smelley and, with two scores, De-Andrew White, a freshman from Houston.

You might want to file this away, if you're keeping track, that White wears No. 2. Like David Palmer.

(Right) Alabama defenders Dont'a Hightower (30), Jesse Williams (54), DeQuan Menzie (24) and Courtney Upshaw (41) crush Vanderbilt quarterback Larry Smith in the first quarter. PHOTO/MARK ALMOND

	1	2	3	4	FINAL
ALABAMA	7	7	13	7	34
VANDERBILT	0	0	0	0	0

TOTAL YARDS

ALABAMA **419**

VANDERBILT **190**

PASSING YARDS

ALABAMA **266**

VANDERBILT **149**

RUSHING YARDS

ALABAMA **153**

VANDERBILT **41**

INDIVIDUAL LEADERS

PASSING	C/ATT	YDS	TD	INT
UA AJ McCarron	23/30	237	4	0
VU Jordan Rodgers	11/18	104	0	2

RUSHING	ATT	YDS	AVG	TD
UA Trent Richardson	19	107	5.6	1
VU Jordan Rodgers	4	23	5.8	0

RECEIVING	REC	YDS	LONG	TD
UA Marquis Maze	9	93	29	0
VU Wesley Tate	3	46	29	0

"It's not about what people's standards are, it's about what our standards are, and our standards are extremely high. It's not about who we're playing. It's about us."

Offensive lineman Barrett Jones

Alabama linebacker Dont'a Hightower (30) congratulates wide receiver DeAndrew White (2) after White's third-quarter touchdown catch.

PHOTO/MARK ALMOND

AP TOP 10	1	2	3	4	5	6	7	8	9	10
10.09.11	LSU	ALABAMA	OKLAHOMA	WISCONSIN	BOISE ST.	OK. ST.	STANFORD	CLEMSON	OREGON	ARKANSAS

A LONG WAY FROM BULLA BULLA

From Australia to Tuscaloosa, Defensive End Jesse Williams is Still a Work in Progress.

By **DON KAUSLER, JR**

TUSCALOOSA — When coaches, teammates and friends talk about how far Jesse Williams has come, they gush. Some refer to distance, others to discipline.

Literally, he has come 9,230 miles to Alabama. It's 7,450 miles from the picturesque beaches of Brisbane on Australia's east coast to the barren desert outside Yuma, Ariz., where he played football for two years at Arizona Western Community College.

And it's 1,780 more miles from Yuma to Tuscaloosa, where he is a starting defensive end this season for the Alabama Crimson Tide.

Figuratively, Williams has come farther. Miles don't measure the distance he has come from a raw talent to a polished player.

Though still a work in progress, Williams is only a few months removed from playing "bulla-bulla ball." That's the term Alabama coach Nick Saban coined in April to describe Williams' lack of technique and training.

Look how far the 6-foot-4, 319-pound Williams has come in just five months.

"Jesse's probably made the most significant improvement from spring practice until now as probably just about any player on our team," Saban said. "He has ability, he has great size, he has good initial quickness, he can run.

"The technical aspects of playing football, the instinctive reactions that you use, how to use your hands, how to pass rush, those kind of things were things that he was a little behind on. But he's a bright guy, he learns really well, he works hard, he wants to be good, he's got a great attitude, so he has made tremendous progress in becoming a good player for us."

Williams played rugby, Australian Rules Football and basketball before he tried football at age 14. Until this year, he was getting by with his significant size, strength, power, quickness and speed.

"Obviously going from junior college and

Australia, my technique was raw and still is," Williams said. "Coming up here to Division I, it's a bit of a reality check with everyone's the same size and I'm just as fast as you. So I think technique is what sets you apart."

Andrew Power was impressed when he saw his best friend from Arizona Western on film Tuesday.

"He's gotten so much better, it's not even funny," Power said. "In the spring, he hadn't really lit the world on fire. I knew this was going to happen when he got some Division I coaching. He was getting better every day at Arizona Western. He's lost a little weight. I knew he was fast, but I didn't know he was that fast. He's just got better technique."

Power traveled 2,340 miles himself from Myrtle Beach, S.C., to play at Arizona Western. Now – it's a small world, after all – Power starts at tight end for North Texas, which means he will try to block Williams on Saturday night when the Mean Green visits Bryant-Denny Stadium.

Alabama defensive lineman Jesse Williams dives for Auburn running back Onterio McCalebb in the second half of Alabama's 42-14 win in the Iron Bowl.

PHOTO/HAL YEAGER

He wouldn't even know what the state was or anything. He'd ask me how good they are, what conference they're in."

They tracked his letters on a dry-erase board and put check marks by the schools that offered scholarships. The check mark next to Alabama came early.

Alabama offensive coordinator Jim McElwain and Arizona Western offensive coordinator Michael Orthmann are close friends. They coached together at Eastern Washington and Montana State.

"That's how Alabama even found Jesse to start with," Power said. "Saban, I mean, he was on him, man. He was recruiting the fool out of the guy."

Williams was "blown away" when he visited Alabama, Power said.

"We might have had about 150 fans out there," Power said of Arizona Western. "I would imagine there weren't too many more than that in Australia.

"I warned him before he went, 'Look, dude, it's going to be crazier than anything you've ever dreamed of.' Coming from the desert where the whole student population shares one weight room and they have one cafeteria, and then you go someplace like Alabama, I said, 'You need to brace yourself for what you're going to see.'"

(Right) Jesse Williams is shown after losing his helmet while making a tackle against Auburn.
PHOTO/MARK ALMOND

It will not be an ordinary challenge.

"He's the best player we had at the junior college, there's no question about it," Power said. "He was just playing with kids. He was making them look stupid.

"He's one of the strongest kids I've ever seen. He's the hardest-working kid I've ever played with."

Power remembers his first impression of Williams.

"When I first got out there, a coach was showing me around, and he said, 'Probably the best player we've got is this Australian kid. He eats paint off the wall,'" Power said.

These friends bonded first because Power had a car. That gave them opportunities to hang out at Wal-Mart. "Jesse likes Wal-Mart a lot," Power said. "There wasn't much else to do there."

Second?

"He figured out that I knew a good amount about college football," said Power, a former walk-on at South Carolina. "He would get offers from people and he wouldn't even know who they were.

(Above) The heavily-tattooed arm of Alabama defensive lineman Jesse Williams is shown during the first practice session of the season. PHOTO/MARK ALMOND

TIDE 52 REBELS 7

Alabama linebacker Nico Johnson reaches out for Ole Miss quarterback Randall Mackey in the first quarter.

PHOTO/MIKE KITTRELL

GRADING THE TIDE

OFFENSE

A

Alabama averaged 9.2 yards on 67 plays. Good blocking helped Trent Richardson. His dazzling 76-yard scoring run was a highlight.

DEFENSE

A

Take away a 72-yard game-opening drive that featured a 59-yard pass, and Ole Miss gained only 69 yards on 47 plays. The Tide had 14 tackles for a loss.

SPECIAL TEAMS

C

The Tide yielded kickoff returns of 47 and 44 yards. Cody Mandell had to punt only once, and his 44-yarder wasn't returned.

COACHING

A

The offensive game plan was to run. The results speak for themselves: 389 yards (9.3 yards per carry).

OVERALL

A

The scary thing for future opponents is that this team hasn't peaked yet. If or when it does, look out.

Assessment by Don Kausler, Jr.

TWO FABLED PERFORMANCES

By **DON KAUSLER, JR.**

OXFORD, Miss. — The defense was the tortoise, Trent Richardson was the hare, and the second-ranked Alabama football team rewrote Aesop with a fabled performance.

The defense started slow but dominated for all but a fraction of a 52-7 victory over Ole Miss.

Richardson was dazzling on a 76-yard touchdown run that highlighted a 183-yard, four-touchdown performance.

And the moral of this mismatch is a strong message to the rest of college football.

"We have yet to put together a full 60 minutes of football," said senior wide receiver Brandon Gibson, who caught the first touchdown pass of his five-year career. "It's a scary feeling. Once we get that down we'll have a lot of fun this season."

Imagine an offense playing better than this: It averaged 9.3 yards per play while compiling 615 total yards (389 rushing).

Picture a defense picking it up after recording 14 tackles for a loss. The nation's top-ranked rushing defense held Ole Miss to 28 yards rushing on 31 carries, thanks to five sacks for 34 yards in losses.

"I thought going in this week they were in the top two or three that we've ever faced," Ole Miss coach Houston Nutt said of the Tide's defense. "But after seeing them live, I think they're much better than seeing them on film. They're much, much better. They're one of the best we've faced in a long, long time."

But this defense wasn't perfect. It surrendered a 59-yard pass on the third play of the game and a touchdown on the fifth play.

After that, Ole Miss netted zero yards on its remaining 18 plays in the first half, which ended with Alabama leading 17-7.

The Tide broke the game open with 28 points in the first 13 minutes of the second half.

"We managed to really hit them in the mouth in the second half," said Richardson, who

opened the half with an 8-yard touchdown run, then followed it with his long, breathtaking run.

On that run, Richardson appeared to hit a dead end inside the 15-yard line, but he froze freshman safety Senquez Golson with a staggering move, then raced into the end zone.

Richardson credited wide receivers Marquis Maze and DeAndrew White with excellent blocks.

"I saw I had to get into the end zone some type of way," said Richardson, who tied Shaun Alexander's school record with a sixth consecutive

"They were telling me to give his ankles back."

Trent Richardson on the reaction of his teammates after a spectacular scoring run that included a stop-and-go move that left a defender on the ground and grasping at air

100-yard game. "I couldn't let those blocks go to waste."

But back to the beginning.

Gibson said the Tide never blinked after falling behind. An 8-yard Richardson TD run capped a nine-play, 79-yard drive on the Tide's first possession.

"When teams come out in the SEC and they give us a nice little blow at the beginning of the game, we've just got to come out with a positive drive, whether it's a field goal or a touchdown," Gibson said.

"Once we get that going and make the ballgame back to (a tie score), it's smooth sailing from there."

(Opposite) Alabama defensive lineman Nick Gentry (58) and Alabama defensive back DeQuan Menzie (24) stop Ole Miss quarterback Randall Mackey in the second quarter. PHOTO/MARK ALMOND

TRAGEDY TO TRIUMPH

RICHARDSON MAKES CASE FOR HEISMAN

By **MIKE HERNDON**

OXFORD, Miss. — Ole Miss is six games into the season and hasn't done many convincing impersonations of an actual defense.

But Trent Richardson should start thinking about what he might say in his Heisman Trophy acceptance speech.

Richardson's performance in Alabama's 52-7 demolition of the Rebels Saturday night was Heisman-worthy. His 183 yards and four touchdowns were both career highs, and those numbers came in less than three quarters.

His 76-yard highlight-reel touchdown run will be replayed on SportsCenter again and again, reminding Heisman voters of what SEC defenders and coaches already know.

"No one has been able to tackle him consistently this year," Ole Miss coach Houston Nutt said. "He should be a Heisman Trophy candidate."

Richardson broke two attempted tackles at the line on that run, then juked Senquez Golson out of his shoes with an ankle-breaking, stop-start move near the goal line to skip into the end zone.

"I saw ol' boy had the corner," Richardson said. "They cut me off at the corner, so I had to try to put a move on him, try to do something to get into the end zone."

Richardson has now run for more than 100 yards in six straight games. His season totals of 912 yards and 15 touchdowns are slightly better than the 905 yards and eight scores Mark Ingram posted through seven games of his Heisman-winning 2009 season.

Richardson didn't see Saturday night's performance as a springboard to the trophy.

"I don't really pay attention to that stuff," he said. "It's been so long since I watched SportsCenter. ... I might have to watch it tonight."

Quarterbacks Andrew Luck of Stanford, Kellen Moore of Boise State and Robert Griffin III of Baylor all threw for more than 300 yards on Saturday.

But the player who may have hurt Richardson's case more than anybody this weekend was Jalston Fowler, whose 125 yards and two TDs put an exclamation point on the statement Richardson started – Ole Miss' defense was no match for anybody wearing crimson.

No matter. Richardson's Heisman candidacy, like the Crimson Tide's season, likely comes down to Nov. 5 at Bryant-Denny Stadium. If he does to LSU what he's done to Alabama's past six opponents, he should get the trophy at midfield after the game.

"I would love that for him," Alabama tackle Barrett Jones said of the thought of Richardson holding the trophy in New York. "He's a great player and he's on the right track."

(Opposite Top) Alabama running back Trent Richardson breaks past Ole Miss defensive tackle Bryon Bennett for a second-quarter touchdown. PHOTO/MARK ALMOND

(Opposite Left) Alabama running back Trent Richardson escapes an Ole Miss defender in the second quarter. PHOTO/MARK ALMOND

(Opposite Right) Alabama running back Trent Richardson laughs as he celebrates Alabama running back Jalston Fowler's 69-yard touchdown in the fourth quarter. PHOTO/MARK ALMOND

	1	2	3	4	FINAL
ALABAMA	7	10	28	7	52
OLE MISS	7	0	0	0	7

TOTAL YARDS
ALABAMA **615**
OLE MISS **141**

PASSING YARDS
ALABAMA 226
OLE MISS **113**

RUSHING YARDS
ALABAMA **389**
OLE MISS **28**

INDIVIDUAL LEADERS

PASSING	C/ATT	YDS	TD	INT
UA AJ McCarron	19/24	224	1	0
UM Randall Mackey	10/21	113	0	1

RUSHING	ATT	YDS	AVG	TD
UA Trent Richardson	17	183	10.8	4
UM Devin Thomas	4	12	3.0	0

RECEIVING	REC	YDS	LONG	TD
UA Darius Hanks	4	63	36	0
UM N. Brassell	3	77	59	0

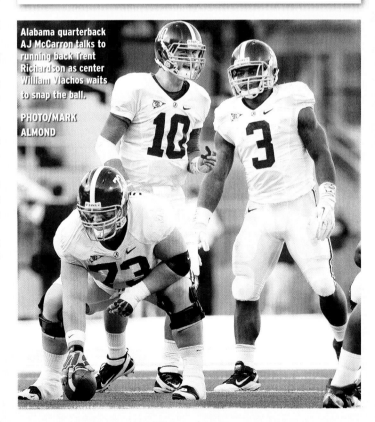

Alabama quarterback AJ McCarron talks to running back Trent Richardson as center William Vlachos waits to snap the ball.

PHOTO/MARK ALMOND

BCS POLL 10.16.11

1	2	3	4	5	6	7	8	9	10
LSU	ALABAMA	OKLAHOMA	OK. ST.	BOISE ST.	WISCONSIN	CLEMSON	STANFORD	ARKANSAS	OREGON

TIDE (37)   VOLUNTEERS (6)

Alabama's Quinton Dial (90) and Courtney Upshaw (41) force Tennessee's Matt Simms to fumble and Ben Bartholomew (39) recovers.

PHOTO/ERIC SCHULTZ

Alabama linebacker Dont'a Hightower celebrates a defensive stop of Tennessee in the third quarter.

PHOTO/MARK ALMOND

GRADING THE TIDE

OFFENSE
B
AJ McCarron (284 yards passing) shined more than RB Trent Richardson.

DEFENSE
A
The Vols didn't reach the end zone; Bama forced three turnovers and held UT to 41 yards and no first downs in the second half.

SPECIAL TEAMS
B
3 for 3 on field goals, including a 45-yarder by Cade Foster, who also had a kickoff for a touchback.

COACHING
B
Whatever came out of Nick Saban's mouth at halftime worked.

OVERALL
B
Bama played down to its level of competition in the first half, then up to LSU's level in the second.

Assessment by Don Kausler, Jr.

BETTER LATE THAN NEVER

By **IZZY GOULD**

TUSCALOOSA — Nick Saban did everything last week short of riding through the streets with a bull horn to warn of a potential slobber-knocking battle with Tennessee.

Alabama's fifth-year head coach barked, shouted and even cursed, trying to snap everyone out of the purple haze coming Nov. 5.

In recent days, it was virtually impossible to avoid hearing of No. 1 LSU's impending visit to Bryant-Denny Stadium to face the second-ranked Crimson Tide in the first No. 1 vs. No. 2 showdown in stadium history.

Whatever happened at halftime Saturday night for this edition of the Third Saturday in October will grow in legend. In reality, Saban flipped a lackluster tie and potential Tennessee upset into another Alabama romp in a 37-6 victory.

"Coach Saban got on our butts," receiver Darius Hanks said after a 6-6 halftime tie. "That's all I can say, really. He told us our whole season depended on this game and we had to get a 'W.'"

The Crimson Tide (8-0, 5-0 SEC) knocked the bolts off of the locker room doors after halftime likely more fearful of the voice that roared through them than the orange nightmare that summed up the first half.

Tennessee (3-4, 0-4) loaded the middle and slowed Heisman Trophy hopeful Trent Richardson, who finished with 17 carries, 77 yards and two touchdowns.

Those plans forced Alabama to turn to sophomore quarterback AJ McCarron and his plethora of wide receivers.

McCarron wasn't himself in the first half after snapping his streak of 152 consecutive passes without an interception when Vols linebacker Austin Johnson picked him off. But he began to find reliable targets such as senior Marquis Maze, who finished with five catches for 106 yards, and began to settle in.

"AJ, I think, got a little bit spooked," Saban said. "They dropped eight guys on him and got the pick early in the game. As the game went on, he played better."

The Crimson Tide pieced together a pair of powerful touchdown drives to begin the third quarter, including a stretch of 10 consecutive first-down plays

(including the touchdowns).

McCarron led a 75-yard drive with four straight first-down passes, then capped it with a 2-yard run in which he ran about 25 yards wide before he plowed into the orange marker to give Alabama a 13-6 lead

Momentum favored the Crimson Tide after it forced a three-and-out highlighted by Courtney Upshaw's sack and forced fumble.

> ## "I'm sure there will be a lot of hype about this game, but I think that everyone needs to chill out mentally, physically and every other way for a few days. We'll have plenty of time to get ready for that game."
>
> *Coach Nick Saban about the Tide's bye week before hosting No. 1 LSU.*

When Alabama got the ball back, McCarron launched a 39-yard TD pass to Kenny Bell to ignite what had been a punch-drunk crowd of 101,821 fans.

McCarron finished 17-of-26 passing for 284 yards, a touchdown, an interception and a sack.

The Crimson Tide's next possession was capped by Richardson's 12-yard TD run through a gauntlet of arms to make it 27-6.

Cade Foster's 45-yard field goal and Richardson's 1-yard scoring run in the fourth quarter made it 37-6.

As the fourth quarter wound down, many of the fans remaining began to chant "L-S-U, L-S-U."

TRAGEDY TO TRIUMPH

BRING ON LSU

Tide Tops Vols to Set Up Top Two Showdown.

By **MARK McCARTER**

TUSCALOOSA — Probably, Nick Saban didn't ask anybody to "excuse my French" at halftime.

Here are your "$20,000 Pyramid" clues.

The middle of a prison riot.

A Kardashian-based reality show.

The Michelle Bachmann campaign committee.

Answer: Places you'd rather be than the Alabama halftime locker room when Saban arrived. You suspect he had little cartoon streams of smoke coming from his ears.

Funny thing, though. When Saban got there, "he didn't bust up nothing," said Courtney Upshaw.

Demonstrating terrific leadership, receiver Marquis Maze already had taken over, reminding his teammates how poorly they played in a somnambulant 6-6 first half. As Dont'a Hightower said, "Sometimes Coach Saban doesn't need to say anything."

Saban, who caused a few ripples earlier in the week by saying a naughty word during his live-in-cyberspace Monday press conference, essentially challenged his players to demonstrate better "energy level, passion, and enthusiasm" in the second half.

"Everybody has to make a commitment to who we are," he told them.

He was stern. The message was pointed. But, Saban said, "It wasn't really an explosion."

Said Saban, "There's no sense in stomping and jumping up and down."

Then, Alabama went and stomped up and down on Tennessee in the second half – with 31 points.

As Alabama swept up late in this 37-6 belated romp over Tennessee, its fans began chanting, "L-S-U! L-S-U!"

You might discover on your calendar that LSU visits Alabama on Nov. 5 for a game between the two top-ranked teams in the country. I suspect we'll have an item or two about that in the paper between now and then.

More than a few observed that the 31-point margin was the same by which the Vols lost to LSU last week.

For the first 30 minutes, this was as far away from a 31-point game as I am from George Clooney.

Alabama rescued itself by stifling Tennessee on its first possession of the second half, then marching 75 yards on a drive that was as resourceful as it was majestic.

When AJ McCarron did a kamikaze dive into the end zone, well, have you ever heard the noise 90,000 people make when they go "Whew!" at the same time?

ALabama's DeAndrew White makes a catch.
PHOTO/ERIC SCHULTZ

	1	2	3	4	FINAL
ALABAMA	3	3	21	10	37
TENNESSEE	3	3	0	0	6

TOTAL YARDS

ALABAMA **437**

TENNESSEE **155**

PASSING YARDS

ALABAMA 294

TENNESSEE **63**

RUSHING YARDS

ALABAMA **143**

TENNESSEE **92**

INDIVIDUAL LEADERS

PASSING	C/ATT	YDS	TD	INT
UA AJ McCarron	17/26	284	1	1
UT M. Simms	8/17	58	0	1
RUSHING	**ATT**	**YDS**	**AVG**	**TD**
UA Trent Richardson	17	77	4.5	2
UT T. Poole	19	67	3.5	0
RECEIVING	**REC**	**YDS**	**LONG**	**TD**
UA Marquis Maze	5	106	69	0
UT T. Poole	3	10	8	0

Former Alabama quarterback Joe Namath greets fans during the game.
PHOTO/ERIC SCHULTZ

Alabama defensive back Vinnie Sunseri (3) celebrates his fourth-quarter fumble recovery. PHOTO/MARK ALMOND

Alabama linebacker Courtney Upshaw celebrates a defensive stop against Kent State in the second quarter.
PHOTO/MARK ALMOND

DRIVEN TO SUCCEED

Who Drives Upshaw Just as Important as What

Alabama linebacker Courtney Upshaw heads for the end zone after intercepting a Florida pass for a touchdown in the second quarter.
PHOTO/G.M. ANDREWS

By **DON KAUSLER, JR.**

EUFAULA — Courtney Upshaw drives a 2002 Buick LaSabre.

What? You were picturing Alabama's eight-cylinder linebacker behind the wheel of a muscle car or a big, honking SUV? Prepare to be surprised.

He saved some Pell Grant money for two years, then made a down payment on the used car in the summer of 2010. He paid sticker, a little more than $5,000. A surrogate father is sure he could have saved Upshaw $500, but negotiating on the student-athlete's behalf would have broken an NCAA rule.

Finally Upshaw had the means to drive himself back and forth between Tuscaloosa and his hometown on a large lake that separates Alabama from Georgia. It's a 200-mile drive one way through the heart of Auburn country to a town that he loves and a town that loves him.

But this story isn't about what a football star drives. It's about what drives a football star.

Most of all, it's about who drives this game-changing football star. This story begins with Upshaw and siblings moving in with an aunt when he was four. He moved around with other relatives, and he didn't have much. Materially, that is.

"Country music stars brag about how poor they were, but a lot of other people don't want other people to know," Eufaula High School football coach Dan Klages said. "I'm not sure how much he wants of that."

Klages is one of many people who have driven Courtney Upshaw.

He didn't see Upshaw's potential instantly. When Upshaw was in the fourth or fifth grade, he attended a camp that Klages was running.

"He was at least half a head taller than the other kids and a decent athlete," Klages said. "I remember thinking, 'Hey, we've got a good one coming down the road.' And then we were playing touch football, and he came up bawling about somebody had punched him, and I thought, 'Oh, my God, he's a big softie. He'll never amount to anything.'"

DRIVING AROUND EUFAULA

Fate put Upshaw in the same kindergarten class with Will McKenzie. One day Will came home and said he was about to get beaten up on the playground.

"Courtney stepped in and told them they'd have to get him, too," recalled Leigh McKenzie, Will's mother, Upshaw's "mother" and a science teacher at Eufaula High.

Soon the boys were best friends. When they were in the second grade, Will told his parents that he wanted to use his Christmas money to register his friend for basketball. Upshaw's aunt, who was raising not only her own children but two nephews and two nieces, said she couldn't get him to all of the practices.

"She agreed that if we would take care of it all, it would be fine," Leigh McKenzie said.

Will's father was the coach.

"I would never tell him this, but he wasn't that good, because his feet were so big," said Tom McKenzie, who went on to coach Upshaw in youth football. "I had no idea that he would be a college athlete."

Upshaw grew to love his second family, but he always has loved his own family, including an older brother and two younger sisters.

"When he was little, I would ask, 'Courtney, what do you want for Christmas?'" Leigh McKenzie recalled. "He'd say, 'Oh, I don't know, but my sister, she loves that baby doll that cries.' If he had money to go shopping, he'd shop for them.

Molly Hagood is another special person in Upshaw's life. She lives across the street from the McKenzies. She was a Eufaula High School guidance counselor who was retired by the time Upshaw became a college football prospect, but she guided him academically nevertheless.

"Those people over there are just remarkable," Hagood said of the McKenzies, whose assistance for Upshaw was cleared by NCAA compliance. "They are not of great wealth. They have educated three very fine children."

Will has older twin sisters who "stay on Courtney like a house on fire," Hagood said.

Upshaw comes back to Eufaula when time allows, and he's treated like a celebrity.

"He's as big as there is," Klages said. "If Elvis came back to life, it might draw a bigger crowd, but I can't think of anybody else."

Upshaw now stays at the McKenzies' house when he's in town, and he always visits the high school and asks if there are any at-risk students he can counsel. He visits with Dewey Norton, a student with cerebral palsy who can't talk but lights up in his wheelchair just at the mention of Upshaw's name. A framed photo of Upshaw and Norton sits on a top shelf of Upshaw's apartment.

Before he left for college, Upshaw asked Eufaula High principal Steve Hawkins how to repay him for everything he had done. Hawkins urged Upshaw to pay it forward.

"For someone who's as ferocious as he is on a football field, I don't know how his heart fits inside his chest," Hawkins said.

TIDE 6   TIGERS 9

Alabama running back Trent Richardson gets tripped up by LSU safety Eric Reid in the first quarter.

PHOTO/MARK ALMOND

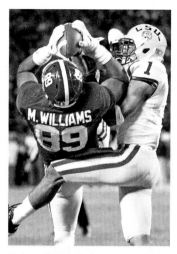

Alabama tight end Michael Williams tries to hold on to an Marquis Maze pass as LSU safety Eric Reid fights him for it.   PHOTO/BILL STARLING

LSU quarterback Jordan Jefferson is sacked behind the line of scrimmage by Alabama defensive lineman Damion Square.   PHOTO/BILL STARLING

Alabama quarterback AJ McCarron looks to pass in the second quarter.
PHOTO/MARK ALMOND

Alabama Coach Nick Saban shows frustration after quarterback AJ McCarron didn't throw to wide-open wide receiver Darius Hanks in the second quarter.
PHOTO/MARK ALMOND

GRADING THE TIDE

OFFENSE

C

The Tide drove into field-goal range five times but came away with only two. A pass picked off at the one was pivotal.

DEFENSE

A

The Tide defense made big stops all night (except once). Two takeaways against a team that had committed three turnovers in eight previous games were excellent.

SPECIAL TEAMS

D

Four missed field goals hurt, and so did Marquis Maze's failure to catch and return a long fourth-quarter punt.

COACHING

B

The Tide tried one trick, and its failure was decisive. Maybe one or more long field goal attempts should have been a punt.

OVERALL

B

So many opportunities were wasted, but it was an epic game against a great opponent.

Assessment by
Don Kausler, Jr.

THE GAME OF THE CENTURY?

By **IZZY GOULD**

TUSCALOOSA — The partying Saturday in anticipation of the biggest game in this town's history impressed generations of fans while attracting plenty of stars.

Gov. Robert Bentley, former Secretary of State Condoleezza Rice and NBA superstar LeBron James, among others, were here to witness an epic defensive battle decided by special teams.

In overtime, No. 1 LSU defeated No. 2 Alabama 9-6 in a game void of touchdowns and settled by kickers.

Some fans said this had a BCS title game feel to it. That's good, considering Alabama's championship hopes are now at the mercy of the BCS system.

"We still have a great opportunity in front of us," Tide center William Vlachos said. "That was a great (LSU) team and our hat is off to them. They beat us tonight and at the same time we can't control our destiny, but we can control what we do from here on out. If we continue to keep the foot on the pedal and get better, I think we have a chance to do something very, very special this season."

LSU is in control not only in the SEC West, but in the battle to reach the BCS national championship game in its backyard.

Once again the Tigers (9-0, 6-0) showed they can win away from Tiger Stadium, eeking out their 10th straight victory.

The winning score came off the foot of LSU kicker Drew Alleman, who kicked a 25-yard field goal and sparked chants of L-S-U, L-S-U. Alleman finished 3-for-3 on field goals, twice to tie the game. He kicked a 30-yard field goal with 14:13 left in the fourth quarter to tie the game at 6. He also made a 19-yarder in the second quarter to tie it at 3.

Neither defense allowed a touchdown in four quarters, letting special teams dictate the outcome.

Alabama's kickers struggled, making just 2-of-6 field goal attempts.

On the first possession of overtime, Alabama was forced to settle for a 52-yard attempt by Cade Foster that fell short. Foster also missed attempts of 44 and 50 yards before he nailed a 46-yarder in the third quarter

for a 6-3 lead.

Tide kicker Jeremy Shelley had a 49-yard attempt blocked before he connected on 34-yarder for a 3-0 lead in the second quarter.

Credit both defenses with limiting scoring chances. Alabama outgained LSU in total yardage 300 to 222.

Alabama was led by linebacker Nico Johnson and his 11 tackles. LSU was led by Ryan Baker's eight tackles, and six each from Eric Reid and Sam Montgomery. Reid also had an interception and forced a fumble. Montgomery registered LSU's only two sacks.

In the middle of it all, Heisman Trophy hopeful

> ## "We knew it was going to be a hard fought game. It just came down to who executed on the chances that they had. They did."
> *Linebacker Courtney Upshaw*

Trent Richardson continued his push with 23 carries for 89 yards and five catches for 80 yards. The Tide's junior running back also returned a kickoff 23 yards.

Both teams had the ball in the final minute of regulation. Alabama forced the Tigers to punt. Alabama ran two plays, electing to play for overtime.

LSU won the toss, forcing Alabama on offense.

AJ McCarron threw two incomplete passes both intended for Richardson, one dropped and one overthrown. Then on third down, he was sacked by Montgomery.

Foster came in to attempt a 52-yard field goal and missed, setting up LSU for the game-winning kick.

BCS POLL	①	②	③	④	⑤	⑥	⑦	⑧	⑨	⑩
11.06.11	LSU	OK. ST.	ALABAMA	STANFORD	BOISE ST.	OKLAHOMA	OREGON	ARKANSAS	CLEMSON	VA. TECH

Alabama running back Trent Richardson is brought down by LSU defensive lineman Quentin Thomas (95) and LSU linebacker Karnell Hatcher (37).
PHOTO/BILL STARLING

GAME OF THE CENTURY: A PREVIEW

By **TOMMY HICKS**

TUSCALOOSA — Even before kickoff of the Game of the Century, there was lots of talk about a possible rematch between the teams in the BCS national championship game.

With Alabama dropping to No. 4 in most of the major polls, but only falling one spot to No. 3 in the only poll that matters – the BCS rankings – that talk continued Sunday night in earnest.

Was Saturday's game merely a warmup for the Game of the Century That Matters?

Or will Oklahoma State win out (it has games against Texas Tech, Iowa State and No. 6 Oklahoma remaining) and end the possibility of LSU-Alabama II? Will LSU be able to remain unbeaten in its final three games (Western Ken-

tucky, Ole Miss and No. 8 Arkansas) and win the SEC championship game? What if Stanford (which plays Oregon this week, with Cal and Notre Dame and probably the Pac-12 title game left) moves up if it remains unbeaten?

Or could the BCS national championship game be a regular-season rematch – of LSU and Oregon?

It seems certain Alabama remains in play for a run at the national title, but there are those who would argue it would not be in the best interest of college football. It could mean having a team that not only didn't win its conference crown, but didn't win its division title playing for the national championship.

Beyond the SEC, there are several teams looking for an opportunity. Oklahoma State, which it would seem controls its own destiny,

leads that group.

Did Saturday's game really settle anything other than the best team in the country (and the SEC) at that moment? And what would a rematch settle? (Other than the national championship, of course.) Or would it?

Based on a number of possible scenarios, there could be split national champions this season.

Want to really get your hypothetical/conspiracy/what-if/anything can happen/wild hair juices flowing? Toss this one around as a possibility: Based on a split national championship and the teams that could be involved, what if LSU and Alabama both won national titles this year?

Yep, it's going to be a crazy few days (and weeks) around the water cooler.

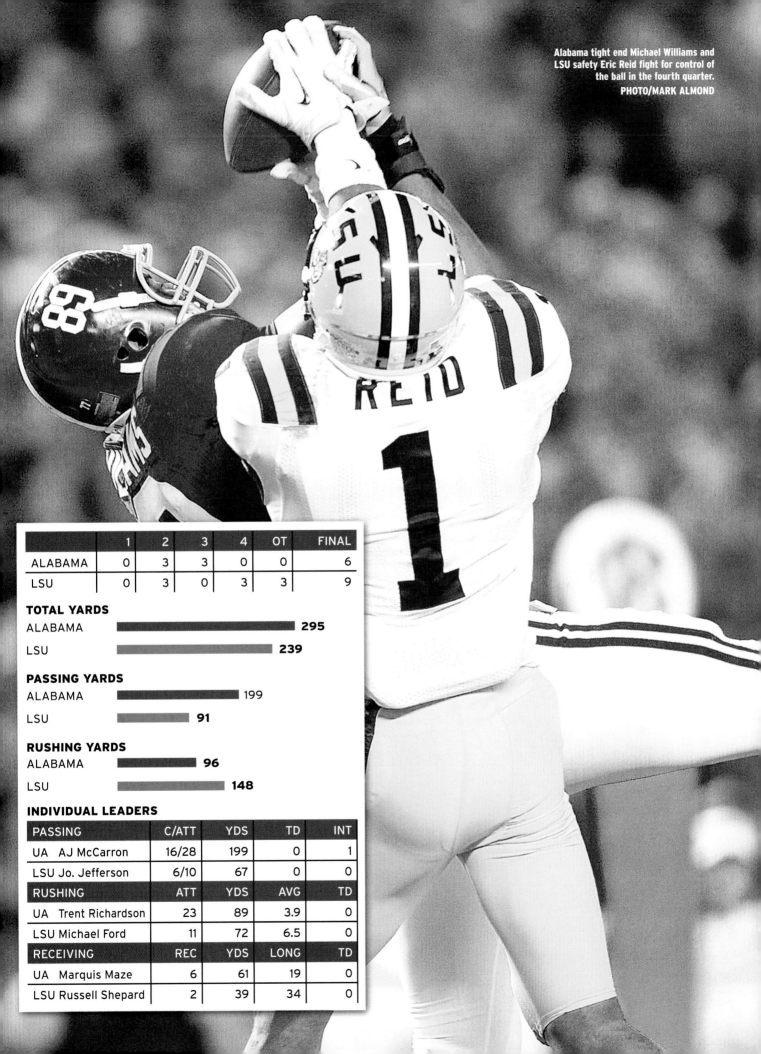

Alabama tight end Michael Williams and LSU safety Eric Reid fight for control of the ball in the fourth quarter.
PHOTO/MARK ALMOND

	1	2	3	4	OT	FINAL
ALABAMA	0	3	3	0	0	6
LSU	0	3	0	3	3	9

TOTAL YARDS
ALABAMA 295
LSU 239

PASSING YARDS
ALABAMA 199
LSU 91

RUSHING YARDS
ALABAMA 96
LSU 148

INDIVIDUAL LEADERS

PASSING	C/ATT	YDS	TD	INT
UA AJ McCarron	16/28	199	0	1
LSU Jo. Jefferson	6/10	67	0	0

RUSHING	ATT	YDS	AVG	TD
UA Trent Richardson	23	89	3.9	0
LSU Michael Ford	11	72	6.5	0

RECEIVING	REC	YDS	LONG	TD
UA Marquis Maze	6	61	19	0
LSU Russell Shepard	2	39	34	0

TIDE 24 BULLDOGS 7

Mississippi State linebacker Deontae Skinner (51) and Mississippi State linebacker Brandon Wilson (58) can't stop Alabama running back Eddie Lacy from scoring in the second quarter.
PHOTO/MARK ALMOND

GRADING THE TIDE

OFFENSE

C

After a slow start, the Tide rolled in the second half, but it converted only 2 of 11 third-down plays, and an interception was almost costly.

DEFENSE

A

The Tide gave up a TD for the first time in 16 quarters but held the Bulldogs to 131 yards (12 rushing on 29 carries).

SPECIAL TEAMS

D

Missed field goals of 49 (Cade Foster) and 31 yards (Jeremy Shelley) extended the Tide's kicking woes. A long kickoff return set up MSU's TD.

COACHING

B

The defense was well-coached throughout. Halftime adjustments helped the offense.

OVERALL

C

With the exception of the defense, the Tide can play better than this.

Assessment by Don Kausler, Jr.

GRINDING OUT A VICTORY

By **IZZY GOULD**

STARKVILLE, Miss. — Alabama's raging response to its first loss apparently was locked in a cage somewhere very far from the clanging cowbells of Davis Wade Stadium.

The Crimson Tide ultimately rescued itself from its deficiencies, thanks in part to Mississippi State's own problems, but mostly once again because of stout defense and its ability to wear out opponents in the second half.

In the end, Alabama pulled out a 24-7 victory in front of 57,871 people, the second-largest crowd ever at Scott Field.

"I'm really pleased and proud of how our players responded in this game," Alabama coach Nick Saban said. "There was a challenge presented to them after a very difficult circumstance a week ago to respond the right way."

The Crimson Tide (9-1, 6-1 SEC) clamped down on the Bulldogs (5-5, 1-5) aided by a tremendous pass rush that kept MSU quarterbacks Chris Relf and Tyler Russell jittery most of the night. Not only did the Tide get plenty of pressure and hits on the quarterbacks, it registered five sacks led by linebacker Dont'a Hightower and his team-high 11 tackles, 1 1/2 sacks and 2 1/2 tackles for loss.

Alabama's defense held the Bulldogs to 131 yards of total offense including just 12 yards of net rushing.

Offensively, the Tide again turned to the running game led by Trent Richardson and his game-high 32 carries for 127 yards and a touchdown. He was aided by sophomore Eddie Lacy, who finished with his second-best statistical performance of the season with 11 carries for 96 yards and two touchdowns.

Lacy's second score was a 32-yard touchdown run

with 1:18 left to put the game away.

"You keep grinding, it's gonna work," Richardson said. "We practice too hard, we work too hard not to win a ballgame like this. When you're in game situations like this, we've gotta keep on grinding."

AJ McCarron finished 14 of 24 for 127 yards and an interception by linebacker Cameron Lawrence, which almost went for a pick six before McCarron re-

> **"It's pretty obvious to anyone that watches them play why they are one of the top two teams in the country."**
>
> *Mississippi State coach Dan Mullen*

grouped to make the tackle at the Tide's 4.

The Bulldogs had already missed a 41-yard attempt by Derek DePasquale, and after the Tide defense stood firm and pushed the Bulldogs back to the 12, he missed a 29-yarder 45 seconds before the half.

Russell later connected with Chris Smith to put the Bulldogs on the scoreboard in the fourth quarter at 17-7 before the Tide locked it down.

(Opposite) Alabama running back Eddie Lacy vaults over Mississippi State defensive back Wade Bonner in the third quarter.
PHOTO/MARK ALMOND

TRAGEDY TO TRIUMPH

BCS POLL	1	2	3	4	5	6	7	8	9	10
11.13.11	LSU	OK. ST.	ALABAMA	OREGON	OKLAHOMA	ARKANSAS	CLEMSON	VA. TECH	STANFORD	BOISE ST.

Alabama linebackers C.J. Mosley (32) and Dont'a Hightower (30) sandwich Mississippi State quarterback Tyler Russell in the third quarter.
PHOTO/MARK ALMOND

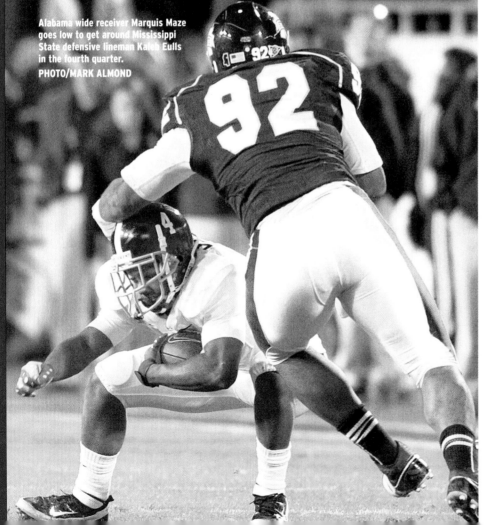

Alabama wide receiver Marquis Maze goes low to get around Mississippi State defensive lineman Kaleb Eulls in the fourth quarter.
PHOTO/MARK ALMOND

TIDE CURES ITS LSU HANGOVER AND CREEPS CLOSER TO REMATCH

	1	2	3	4	FINAL
ALABAMA	0	7	3	14	24
MISSISSIPPI	0	0	0	7	7

TOTAL YARDS

ALABAMA **386**

MSU **131**

PASSING YARDS

ALABAMA 163

MSU **119**

RUSHING YARDS

ALABAMA **223**

MSU **12**

INDIVIDUAL LEADERS

PASSING	C/ATT	YDS	TD	INT
UA AJ McCarron	14/24	163	0	1
MSU Tyler Russell	13/25	110	1	0
RUSHING	ATT	YDS	AVG	TD
UA Trent Richardson	32	127	4	1
MSU Vick Ballard	9	21	2.3	0
RECEIVING	REC	YDS	LONG	TD
UA Marquis Maze	4	22	13	0
MSU Chris Smith	5	42	16	1

Alabama linebackers C.J. Mosley and Dont'a Hightower celebrate their sack of Mississippi State quarterback Tyler Russell in the third quarter.
PHOTO/MARK ALMOND

By **KEVIN SCARBINSKY**

STARKVILLE, Miss. — If you're a title contender who just lost a 15-round split decision, and you have to fight again the next week, there's no better place to climb back in the ring than Davis-Wade Stadium.

Nothing cures a hangover like – wait for it – a little hair of the Bulldog.

Think about it.

Dan Mullen, the alleged brains behind Urban Meyer's old operation, is in the home stretch of his third season at Mississippi State.

How many conference games has State won this season? One. At Kentucky. Which really doesn't count unless the ball is round. How many division games has State won against teams not named Ole Miss since Mullen took over? None.

Not one.

Alabama was not going to be the first.

"They're definitely one of the top two teams in the country," Mullen said after seeing the evidence in person. Alabama 24, Mississippi State 7 was a demonstration.

Mullen's Bulldogs may never find themselves in a better position to catch Nick Saban's Crimson Tide in the right place at the right time. Alabama

wasn't in a good place physically or emotionally a week after dropping that overtime decision at home to LSU.

Suffering a close loss in the game of the century can be one of the leading causes of suffering the upset of the year. After losing control of its championship destiny, not to mention its best blocker and team leader, wounded Barrett Jones, who dressed but didn't play, the visitors limped into the teeth of the second-largest crowd in the history of Davis-Wade Stadium. A combination of 57,871 people and 57,871 cowbells, give or take, can get in your head.

No matter. The best defense in college football can clear your head in a hurry.

If Alabama didn't score in the first 15 minutes, Mississippi State got blanked for the first three quarters. Before the Bulldogs located the scoreboard for the first and only time early in the fourth quarter, they found themselves behind by three scores.

Alabama may have missed two more field goals, and AJ McCarron's biggest contribution may have been a tackle on an interception that prevented a pick six and a tie late in the second quarter, but this wasn't about perfection. Perfection became an impossible dream last week.

This was about fighting through the kind of

game a team still in title contention has to win, especially on a day when two other teams in the also-needing-help category go down.

Boise State should be kicking itself after its 36-35 home loss to TCU. For the second straight season, the Broncos missed a would-be game-winning field goal at the finish to watch their undefeated season and championship hopes vanish. There goes the debate between a one-loss SEC heavy and a no-loss non-automatic qualifier darling.

If that wasn't enough good news for the Crimson Nation, Oregon made sure the Pac-12 won't have an undefeated champion by cutting down Stanford 53-30. Can you say tim-ber?

That opens another discussion. Who would be more deserving of a rematch with No. 1 LSU in the BCS Championship Game – Alabama or Oregon? Alabama lost to LSU close at home. Oregon lost to LSU big at a neutral site. Advantage, Alabama.

But that's only if LSU, Alabama and Oregon all win out. And Oklahoma State doesn't. The No. 2 Cowboys, who just wiped the smirk off Tommy Tuberville's face 66-6, look more and more like this year's version of Auburn 2010. Alabama needs a little more help from its friends. Its defense will do the rest.

TIDE 45   EAGLES 21

SABAN: 'I'M GLAD IT'S OVER'

By **IZZY GOULD**

TUSCALOOSA — Georgia Southern's offensive style was a throwback like its uniforms.

The Eagles were masters of the triple option, a style of football perhaps more fitting for black-and-white television than pay-per view HD. They offered the nation's top-ranked defense a pop quiz of sorts, forcing the Crimson Tide to show more brains than brawn.

Alabama prevailed with a 45-21 victory to close out the home slate of the 2011 season at Bryant-Denny Stadium. The win was necessary

for the Tide (10-1), ranked third in the BCS standings, to keep its hopes of a national championship berth alive.

Alabama's victory wasn't fit for the Louvre, but most outsiders will simply glance at the numbers and assume the obvious — Alabama took care of business. But the score wasn't indicative of the tight contest, which was a 10-point game for most of the third quarter and forced the Tide to use its starters deep into the fourth.

Georgia Southern's offensive decisions on fourth down resembled a Las Vegas high roller with a nothing-to-lose mentality fueled by 18

carries, 153 yards and a touchdown from freshman Dominique Swope.

Twice, the Eagles converted fourth downs to extend drives. The first led to a score – a fourth-and-1 from the Eagles' 29-yard line that quarterback Jaybo Shaw hammered up the middle. Five plays later, Shaw connected with Jonathan Bryant on a 39-yard catch and run to make it 24-14 in favor of the Tide.

In the fourth quarter, Georgia Southern would go 11 plays and 70 yards to the Tide's 8-yard line when Tide safety Mark Barron made a big stop on quarterback Jerick McKinnon as he

found open space on a run to the right but picked up just 1 yard.

Then on fourth-and-5, Shaw threw an incomplete pass in the back of the end zone. Tide cornerback DeQuan Menzie broke up the pass intended for Mitchell Wilford.

Alabama would eat all but 44 seconds on its final drive, capped by a 4-yard touchdown pass from Alabama sophomore AJ McCarron to tight end Brad Smelley, who made a one-handed grab. It was the second touchdown catch for the Tuscaloosa native, who was celebrating senior day and his final home game. His first was a 34-yard touchdown

from McCarron to give the Tide a 31-14 led in the third quarter.

"I would hope so," Smelley said when asked if he could envision scoring two touchdowns in his final home game. "That's never happened before, so I wasn't anticipating it. It was great to make a couple of plays for the team."

Early on, it appeared Alabama was prepared to roll to another lopsided victory without stretching its legs.

The Tide jumped out to a 17-0 lead thanks to a 32-yard field goal by Jeremy Shelley, a punt block by Dont'a Hightower scooped up and returned 55

yards by Dre Kirkpatrick, and a 4-yard pass from McCarron to running back Trent Richardson.

The junior continued to add to his Heisman Trophy resume, matching a career-high 32 carries with 175 yards and two touchdowns on the ground. He also set Alabama's single-season touchdown record with 20 for the year.

After a 1-yard touchdown run put Alabama ahead 24-7 in the second quarter, Richardson set the record with a 1-yard touchdown run in the third for a 38-21 lead.

TRAGEDY TO TRIUMPH

113

Alabama running back Trent Richardson leaps into the end zone for a 1-yard touchdown in the second quarter.

PHOTO/MARK ALMOND

FOOTBALL GODS MUST WANT ALABAMA-LSU REMATCH

By **JON SOLOMON**

TUSCALOOSA — We're spoiled rotten in this state. We know it.

Alabama's undefeated regular season in 2008. Alabama's national title and Mark Ingram's Heisman Trophy in 2009. Auburn's national title and Cam Newton's Heisman in 2010.

And just when it appeared the 2011 Iron Bowl would arrive without one of the participants controlling its national title fate, Paul Rhoads sent a gift from Ames, Iowa. When we last saw Rhoads as Auburn's talented, one-year defensive coordinator in 2008, he was on the losing end of the last Iron Bowl blowout, which ushered out Tommy Tuberville and brought in Iowa State's Gene Chizik.

Alabama now needs Rhoads' address to send holiday cards. Fruit baskets will be accepted, too.

"Absolutely mayhem in hotel capstone," Alabama offensive lineman Barrett Jones posted on Twitter on Friday night after Rhoads guided Iowa State to an upset of No. 2 Oklahoma State. "Everyone in the halls hugging each other. Now WE control our destiny."

Or as safety Vinnie Sunseri put it: "We told everyone to believe!!! Roll Cyclones Roll!!!"

It's not every day an Alabama fan chooses to bring an Iowa State shirt to Bryant-Denny Stadium, much less draw the loudest, in-your-gut, primal scream from the crowd when the man was shown on the scoreboard. But then it's not every day you get second chances in college football's convoluted postseason system.

Now what does Alabama do with theirs?

The Crimson Tide, now No. 2 in the BCS standings. All that non-stop speculation about an Alabama-LSU rematch isn't a pipe dream. It's extremely close to reality.

Alabama's good fortunes continued late Saturday night. It's as if the college football gods have ordained an Alabama-LSU rematch.

Oregon is done from the BCS title race after losing to USC. The Ducks couldn't get past the Trojans at home, thanks to questionable clock management at the end by Chip Kelly. Mike Slive has never cheered so much for Lane Kiffin.

With new life, will Alabama now be concerned about margin of victory against Auburn? Don't bet against it. On Saturday against Georgia Southern, AJ McCarron threw a 4-yard touchdown pass with 44 seconds left and Alabama ahead 38-21.

Unless Gus Malzahn can teach wishbone tendencies to Auburn in one week, Alabama need not fret about Georgia Southern's 302 rushing yards.

"We're not worried about the national championship," Alabama coach Nick Saban said, veering into a rant about staying focused. "We're worried about our next game."

For the fourth straight season, that next game isn't just for local bragging rights. The state championship that used to be about counting Tuberville's fingers continues to accumulate national title dreams.

Pinch us. We'll wake up one of these years.

Alabama running back Trent Richardson tries to get past Georgia Southern linebacker Josh Rowe in the third quarter. PHOTO/MARK ALMOND

	1	2	3	4	FINAL
ALABAMA	10	14	14	7	45
GA SOUTHERN	0	14	7	0	21

TOTAL YARDS
ALABAMA 462
GSU 341

PASSING YARDS
ALABAMA 190
GSU 39

RUSHING YARDS
ALABAMA 272
GSU 302

INDIVIDUAL LEADERS

PASSING	C/ATT	YDS	TD	INT
UA AJ McCarron	14/19	190	3	0
GSU J. Shaw	1/5	39	1	0
RUSHING	ATT	YDS	AVG	TD
UA Trent Richardson	32	175	5.5	2
GSU D. Swope	18	153	8.5	1
RECEIVING	REC	YDS	LONG	TD
UA Brad Smelley	4	58	34	2
GSU J. Bryant	1	39	39	1

Alabama wide receiver Brandon Gibson breaks away from Georgia Southern cornerback Hudson Presume on a first-quarter pass.
PHOTO/MARK ALMOND

"Right now, things are going in our fortune, and we've just got to finish out the season and hope for the best."

Linebacker Dont'a Hightower after a weekend in which No. 2 Oklahoma State lost and Alabama moved back into strong national championship contention

BCS POLL										
11.20.11	1 LSU	2 ALABAMA	3 ARKANSAS	4 OK. ST.	5 VA. TECH	6 STANFORD	7 BOISE ST.	8 HOUSTON	9 OKLAHOMA	10 OREGON

ALABAMA'S FOOTBALL TEAM WINS DISNEY SPIRIT AWARD FOR OUTREACH DURING TUSCALOOSA TORNADO RECOVERY

Alabama snapper Carson Tinker congratulates Alabama kicker Jeremy Shelley after his field goal in the second quarter against LSU.   PHOTO/MARK ALMOND

By MARK McCARTER

TUSCALOOSA — Leave the campus and head up the bumpy street toward the railroad tracks. Stop. Wait. Sit as the crossing bar all but drops in your lap, letting Amtrak's Crescent rumble south toward New Orleans.

It's the same destination, the site of the BCS Championship Game, for Alabama's football team, if all goes well for the Tide this weekend.

It's a different world on the other side of the tracks. The stately University of Alabama buildings and healthy trees and sense of normalcy in your rear-view mirror give way to a wasteland.

But, because of what a football team did off the field as much as on it, there is an unbreakable sense of community that connects the two sides.

Stories are legion about how Alabama's football players, and many other Tide coaches, athletes and former athletes, assisted in the tornado recovery effort.

For that, the 2011 Alabama football team was announced Monday as the winner of the Disney Spirit Award. It's been given annually since 1996 to college football's most inspirational player or team.

"It really speaks well for the University of Alabama," coach Nick Saban said. "It speaks well for a lot of people in the organization who made a significant contribution to trying to help a community that was affected by probably as devastating of a circumstance as I've ever had to deal with in my life."

Carson Tinker, the Tide's long snapper, will accept the award on behalf of his teammates.

Tinker, said Saban, "probably lost the most and has given the most."

Tinker's girlfriend, Ashley Harrison, was yanked out of his arms and killed when the tornado struck his home.

Acres upon acres still sit empty after April's tornadoes in Tinker's old Forest Lake neighborhood. Massive signposts that once hoisted neon messages stretch empty-handed into the sky. A peaceful lake remains littered with limbs and debris.

Blue tarps still protect dozens of tattered roofs. Professionally printed and crudely painted signs proclaim the same message:

"We're Coming Back."

Deep in the pit of your stomach, you wonder if they really can. There is still a day-after feel in some places. You can sense the helpless "where are we supposed to start?" feeling so many tornado victims have articulated.

It's one tiny step at a time. The guys with the post-hole diggers planting some landscaping at a house that's nearly habitable again. A block away, a guy with the bulldozer shoving away construction debris. Painters another block away.

On many of the homes, crimson Alabama flags hang limply from porch columns.

"I know our community cares about us a lot," offensive lineman William Vlachos said. "I don't think what we do on Saturdays necessarily heals people and what they've gone through. But any time you can distract and entertain, which is what we do, that's very important."

Back across the tracks, part of Saban's weekly news conference was about Alabama's mindset. After its emotional loss to LSU, the Tide has been lackluster in easy wins over Mississippi State and Georgia Southern.

Even on Iron Bowl week, the sentiment that a football team is coming back seems awfully trite on the other side of the tracks. Then again, maybe it's simply part of the shared spirit of this bruised community.

Alabama's Aaron Douglas.
PHOTO/KENT GIDLEY

By **IZZY GOULD**

TUSCALOOSA — The clothes still embrace his scent.

Journals preserve his handwriting, and the words reveal the creative flow of his mind.

Each time Karla Douglas and David Douglas begin packing away his room, vivid memories of their son open their emotions.

Karla seeks therapy. David goes hunting to think. Five months after Aaron Douglas died from a drug overdose at a house party in Florida, his parents still weep often for their son.

Aaron was an offensive lineman at Alabama when he died May 12, his body discovered on a second-floor balcony after a random visit to a house party in Fernandina Beach, Fla., where he was vacationing.

The thought of Aaron alone in his most vul-nerable moment has been difficult for his parents to grasp.

Aaron was 21, but had always been "Momma's boy," Karla said. He once said in a song to his father, "Pops, you're the man for always hav-ing my back."

"He died all alone on that balcony," Karla said, "and we were not there to help him."

Aaron wanted to earn a college degree and play in the NFL. At 6-foot-7, 275 pounds, he was a physical phenomenon with enough talent to compete for the starting offensive left tackle spot at Alabama. After start-ing his career at Tennessee, he would have been at the center of attention during the Third Saturday in October rivalry week.

Aaron also challenged himself through music, pen-ning rap lyrics he could pound out through his mouth. He hoped one day to own a re-cording studio.

Football and music were his passions, and he would cling to them living in the sparse desert landscape of Yuma, Arizona, one of the na-tion's small border towns in the southwest corner of Ari-zona on the California border.

This was the place where he would wrestle back control of his world.

"His decision to go 1,989 miles away from home was a welcoming chal-lenge," Karla said. "He grew as a player and a per-son, and we saw a young man excited about life and football again."

On the field, he earned All-American honors recruiting interest from some of the nation's top programs. The process energized Aaron because he never truly experienced it coming out of high school. Most programs assumed he was a lock for Tennessee.

Aaron ultimately signed with Alabama last winter and joined Matadors' teammate Jesse Wil-liams, who is a starting defensive end with the Crimson Tide.

"We were friends in junior college," Williams said last month. "After transferring here, we kind of stuck together."

Aaron was brought to Alabama to compete for the starting left tackle position vacated by two-year starter James Carpenter, now with the Seattle Seahawks. He competed throughout the spring with Alfred McCullough.

After three weeks, Alabama experimented with Barrett Jones, who made the move from right guard. Few could have anticipated the move would stick, especially due to circumstances out of their control.

"I still think about it when I see the locker," Jones said. "It's weird to see him gone."

This week, Aaron's parents will attend the Third Saturday in October wearing crimson and white.

They anxiously anticipated the day they would watch their son face their alma mater for the first time playing for Alabama.

Alabama is wearing black stickers on its hel-mets with Aaron's No. 77, and the media guide has a portrait of Aaron on Page 3, the years of his life 1989-2011 below. The school also has left his locker vacant.

"I never had a player die before," Saban said in July. "I have a tremendous amount of respect and a completely different feeling talking in front of our team now. Maybe you take it for granted that they're all always going to be there. It's prob-ably the same thing with your children at home if you've ever lost one. These things all have a tre-mendous impact and change the perspective of things."

Karla understands that as well as anyone.

"For the first few weeks after his death, I put his cologne on one of his favorite hoodies and slept with it," she said. "I have two shirts in my closet to see and touch and I have listened to many of his songs, so I can hear his voice.

One of the songs, 'Keep Your Head High,' played at his service, Aaron says, 'Momma I love you and you have your son back.' This brings comfort along with tears."

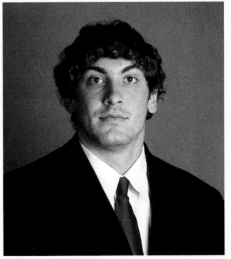

PHOTO/KENT GIDLEY

Alabama linebacker Courtney Upshaw sacks Auburn quarterback Clint Moseley in the second quarter.

PHOTO/MARK ALMOND

Alabama defensive lineman
Jesse Williams loses his
helmet as he and Alabama
linebacker Courtney
Upshaw (41) sack Auburn
quarterback Kiehl Frazier in
the second quarter.

PHOTO/MARK ALMOND

GRADING THE TIDE

OFFENSE

A

QB AJ McCarron was sharp, especially on third down. RB Trent Richardson was strong (203 rushing yards). The line wore Auburn down.

DEFENSE

A

Auburn's offense didn't score. It converted 3-of-15 third downs and had only 140 total yards.

SPECIAL TEAMS

B

A kickoff return for a TD for a second consecutive week was alarming. Otherwise, 2-for-2 on field goals by Jeremy Shelley, two touchbacks on kickoffs by Cade Foster, and three punts by Cody Mandell for a 40.3-yard average were highlights.

COACHING

A

The offensive plan showed imagination on a handoff-pitchback-touchdown pass, and a 2-point conversion with left tackle Barrett Jones split wide as a decoy receiver was well-conceived and well-executed.

OVERALL

A

The Crimson Tide dominated everywhere but the scoreboard until the fourth quarter. Then it finished.

Assessment by Don Kausler, Jr.

THE LOOK OF REVENGE

By **DON KAUSLER, JR.**

AUBURN — A year after Auburn showed the gleaming eye of the Tiger during a tenacious comeback from a 24-0 deficit to an improbable, unforgettable 28-27 victory, this was the eye of the Tide.

This was a stare. This was a glare. This was a dare.

Forget about Courtney Upshaw watching the faces of Auburn players in the fourth quarter and seeing a different look from them. The Tide was showing a different look, too.

"I'm sure they saw the look in my eyes and the rest of my teammates' eyes," Alabama's senior outside linebacker said. "We had that dominating look."

The scoreboard at Jordan-Hare Stadium also had a different look, and it too said domination. Alabama 42, Auburn 14.

Many stars helped the No. 2 Crimson Tide (11-1, 7-1 in the Southeastern Conference) move into position for a BSC Championship Game berth and rematch with No. 1 LSU.

Trent Richardson made a Heisman Trophy statement with 203 yards running and a touchdown catch. AJ McCarron competed 18 of 23 passes for 184 yards and three first-half touchdowns. Brad Smelley caught six passes for 86 yards, one for a touchdown and five for a third- or fourth-down conversion.

But on a day when "D" stood for determination as well as domination, the nation's No. 1 defense stood above all.

"We played probably one of the best defensive games we've played all year," said inside linebacker Dont'a Hightower, who led Alabama with nine tackles.

And that's saying something. The nation's top scoring defense (8.36 points per game) didn't allow a point. Auburn's defense recovered a fumble for a touchdown, and Onterio McCalebb started the second half by running 83 yards for Auburn's first Iron Bowl kickoff return for a touchdown.

The nation's top rushing defense (74.6 yards per game) held Auburn (7-5, 4-4) to 78 yards rushing. Mike Dyer, the No. 2 rusher in the SEC, ran 13 times for 48 yards, 60 yards fewer than his average.

"The game plan was to eliminate the run game," Hightower said. "We were able to win up front and have our linebackers play aggressive."

The nation's No. 1 passing defense (121.3 yards per game) held Auburn to 62 yards, and Dee Milliner returned an interception 35 yards for a touchdown early

in the fourth quarter to help the Tide pull away to a 35-14 lead.

That's 140 total yards against a defense that was leading the nation in total yards allowed at 195.9. Auburn converted only 3-of-15 third-down plays, and Alabama made two fourth-down stops.

"They were tough to block up front, whether it was run blocking or pass blocking," Auburn coach Gene

> "There were a lot of guys saying the 'Never Again' slogan. Me personally, I told them, 'This is just another team in the way. We're here for one thing, and that's to get that W.'"
>
> *Linebacker Courtney Upshaw on the slogan that had reminded Tide players of the previous season's collapse against Auburn*

Chizik said. "They are just a really good defense. You don't become the No. 1 defense in the country in about every category by accident."

Like last year, Alabama scored two touchdowns quickly. Like last year, the Tide led 24-7 at halftime. Like last year, the Tigers started to come back with McCalebb's kickoff return.

But the Tide asserted itself offensively and defensively in the fourth quarter.

What made junior cornerback Dre Kirkpatrick prouder than anything?

"How we finished," he said. "We stayed strong, and the defense didn't give up any touchdowns."

Before turning their attention to the BCS Championship Game on Jan. 9 in New Orleans, first there was a chance for players to savor sweet revenge.

"More important than the national championship game was us concentrating on last year," Hightower said. "We waited 365 days to get this game back."

BCS POLL	1	2	3	4	5	6	7	8	9	10
11.27.11	LSU	ALABAMA	OK. ST.	STANFORD	VA. TECH	HOUSTON	BOISE ST.	ARKANSAS	OREGON	OKLAHOMA

BIG EASY

Alabama crushes Auburn in Iron Bowl to state case for spot in BCS championship game in NewOrleans

By **RANDY KENNEDY**

AUBURN — Never again.

For 364 days, Alabama's players had been forced to look at a poster with those words emblazoned over a photo of Auburn stars Cam Newton and Nick Fairley celebrating an unlikely and dramatic comeback from a 24-7 halftime deficit in Tuscaloosa last season.

On Saturday at Jordan-Hare Stadium, the Crimson Tide again led 24-7 at halftime. And just like a year earlier, the Tigers scored early in the third quarter to cut Alabama's lead to 24-14.

But that's where the similarities ended.

Never again? Maybe not. But a similar collapse in the foreseeable future is very unlikely for a program that has lost only once in 13 games since the Crimson Collapse.

The 2011 Crimson Tide team showed again Saturday that it is nothing like the 2010 team that was talented but not always mentally tough. And the 2011 Auburn Tigers bear no resemblance to the squad that won the national championship just 10 months ago.

To say these two programs have gone in opposite directions since last season is like saying the BCS formula can be kind of confusing.

While Auburn is headed to the kind of second-tier bowl offered to a team that was blown out by at least 24 points four times in conference play this season, Alabama has staked a strong claim to play for the BCS national championship in New Orleans.

"I feel like we have a great football team," Crimson Tide coach Nick Saban said in addressing the possibility that Alabama could get a rematch with LSU for the national title. "I believe they deserve an opportunity."

Here's how dominant Alabama was against Auburn:

The Crimson Tide gave up a kickoff return for a touchdown and a defensive score, yet still easily covered the largest point spread in Iron Bowl history (20½ points).

Auburn's longest play from scrimmage through the first three quarters was 7 yards.

Mike Dyer ran for only 48 yards on 13 carries. And he was the Tigers' offensive star of the game.

Alabama seemed able to throw the ball at will, yet attempted only 5 passes (4 complete for 20 yards) after halftime. For Auburn, those numbers are disappointingly similar to those posted by Georgia in cruising to an easy win over the Tigers.

Four years ago, the Iron Bowl was played in Auburn, with the Tigers winning 17-10. That was the week of the return of the Textbook Five and Saban's rude initiation into the rivalry. It was also the sixth win in a row in the series for Tommy Tuberville and the dominating Tigers.

Since then, Alabama has posted two Iron Bowl blowouts by an average score of 39-7, won a great game on the way to the 2009 national championship, and lost by one point on a remarkable rally by the 2010 national champion Tigers.

This rivalry, the best in country, hasn't turned to the point that anyone should be saying "never again," but there's no doubt which program is on more solid footing at this point.

It's the one that will be playing in the BCS championship game in January.

Auburn tight end Philip Lutzenkirchen gets flipped over Alabama defensive back Dee Milliner in the fourth quarter.

PHOTO/MARK ALMOND

	1	2	3	4	FINAL
ALABAMA	14	10	3	15	42
AUBURN	7	0	7	0	14

TOTAL YARDS

ALABAMA **397**

AUBURN **140**

PASSING YARDS

ALABAMA **184**

AUBURN **62**

RUSHING YARDS

ALABAMA **213**

AUBURN **78**

INDIVIDUAL LEADERS

PASSING	C/ATT	YDS	TD	INT
UA AJ McCarron	18/23	184	3	0
AU Clint Moseley	11/18	62	0	1
RUSHING	ATT	YDS	AVG	TD
UA Trent Richardson	27	203	7.5	0
AU Michael Dyer	13	48	3.7	0
RECEIVING	REC	YDS	LONG	TD
UA Brad Smelley	6	86	35	1
AU Quan Bray	5	22	7	0

Alabama tight end Brad Smelley catches a second quarter pass in front of Auburn defensive back Ryan Smith.

PHOTO/MARK ALMOND

Alabama linebacker Alex Watkins celebrates after tackling Auburn's Quan Bray on a fourth quarter kick return.

PHOTO/MARK ALMOND

Alabama coach Nick Saban acknowledges the fans after Alabama's 42-14 win. PHOTO/HAL YAEGER

Alabama running back Trent Richardson carries the ball in the fourth quarter against Mississippi State.

PHOTO/MARK ALMOND

AFTER RECORD-BREAKING SEASON ALABAMA'S RICHARDSON FINISHES THIRD

By **IZZY GOULD**

NEW YORK — Robert Griffin III's Superman socks were more stunning than the outcome of the 77th Heisman Trophy ceremony.

"This is unbelievably believable," Griffin III said. "To Baylor nation, I say this is a forever moment, may we be blessed enough to have more of these in the future."

Baylor's quarterback won the award soundly as predicted, beating out the field including Stanford quarterback Andrew Luck, who is now a two-time Heisman Trophy runner-up. Trent Richardson finished third after visiting New York for the first time as Alabama's second Heisman finalist in three years.

Wisconsin's Montee Ball finished fourth, and LSU's Tyrann Mathieu finished fifth.

Afterward, Richardson was asked plenty of questions including how could he possibly top Griffin's socks?

"Try to be Superman in the LSU game," Richardson said. "We've got that coming up."

Richardson said his attention is now squarely on preparation for the rematch with LSU on Jan. 9 in the BCS Championship Game in New Orleans.

Voting results were distributed to reporters mere seconds after Griffin had learned he had won.

Perhaps most telling was how the voting went in the South region. Griffin took the South, and all but one region – the Far West, which was won by Luck.

Richardson was third in all but one region. He had 256 points in the South, which was led by Griffin's 303 points.

Overall, Griffin had the most first-place votes (405) and totaled 1,687 points. Luck had 247 first-place votes and totaled 1,407 points. Richardson had 138 first-place votes and finished with 978 points.

Throughout the past week, Heisman analysts have projected the winner by gathering ballot information released by various voters. Griffin was projected by most to be the favorite, so much so the betting lines moved last week making him the favorite.

Griffin's numbers were certainly Heisman worthy. He threw for 3,998 yards, 36 touchdowns and just six interceptions. He also had 161 carries for 644 yards and nine touchdowns. Some have argued Alabama's absence from the SEC championship game hurt Richardson's chances not playing the final weekend.

Meanwhile, Baylor rolled to a 48-24 win over Texas in the final weekend with Griffin throwing for 320 yards and two touchdowns while rushing for two more leaving a lasting impression two days before votes were due.

Richardson was asked if he entered the ceremony believing Griffin had won.

"Yeah, that's always been in my head," Richardson said. "They did play that last game, and he did play an awesome game. ... That dude is awesome. I'm happy for him."

Once it was over, Richardson said he had at least 100 text messages pile up on his iPhone. He said he received messages from Pensacola icons Emmitt Smith and Roy Jones Jr., congratulating him on being a finalist and showing their support.

While Griffin made his way to a press conference, the others went to the ninth floor of the Marriott Marquis in Times Square to meet with reporters.

Those interviews took place near a glass balcony overlooking a hotel restaurant. Once patrons realized four of the Heisman finalists were above them, they began shouting for their attention.

Richardson stepped to the railing and people cheered while snapping photographs with cell phones and cameras. Then he let out a "Roll Tide."

"I don't feel like I lost anything," Richardson said. "There was nothing to lose. It happened like it happened. He's a great player. ... I'm just happy to be here, and have my name in this race."

HERE'S THE FINAL NATIONAL VOTE RANKING:

Rank	Player	School	Position	1st Place Votes	Total Points
1	Robert Griffin III	Baylor	QB	405	1687
2	Andrew Luck	Stanford	QB	247	1407
3	Trent Richardson	Alabama	RB	138	978
4	Montee Ball	Wisconsin	RB	22	348
5	Tyrann Mathieu	LSU	DB	34	327
6	Matt Barkley	USC	QB	11	153
7	Case Keenum	Houston	QB	10	123
8	Kellen Moore	Boise State	QB	6	90
9	Russell Wilson	Wisconsin	QB	4	52
10	LaMichael James	Oregon	RB	5	48

TRAGEDY TO TRIUMPH

ALABAMA'S FINAL SEASON STATISTICS*

OFFENSE

RUSHING

	GP	ATT	GAIN	LOSS	NET	AVG	TD	LG	AVG/G
Trent Richardson	13	283	1740	61	1679	5.9	21	76	129.2
Eddie Lacy	12	95	694	20	674	7.1	7	67	56.2
Jalston Fowler	13	56	395	10	385	6.9	4	69	29.6
Blake Sims	5	22	126	19	107	4.9	0	45	21.4
Brad Smelley	13	1	1	0	1	1.0	0	1	0.1
Marquis Maze	13	6	7	13	-6	-1.0	0	6	-0.5
Phillip Sims	8	5	15	25	-10	-2.0	0	15	-1.2
AJ McCarron	13	30	50	72	-22	-0.7	2	13	-1.7

PASSING

	GP	EFFIC	COMP	ATT	INT	PCT	YDS	TD	LG	AVG/G
AJ McCarron	13	147.3	219	328	5	66.8	2634	16	69	202.6
Phillip Sims	8	98.9	18	28	2	64.3	163	0	19	20.4
Marquis Maze	13	-200.0	0	1	1	0.0	0	0	0	0.0

RECEIVING

	GP	NO.	YDS	AVG	TD	LG	AVG/G
Marquis Maze	13	56	627	11.2	1	69	48.2
Brad Smelley	13	34	356	10.5	4	35	27.4
Trent Richardson	13	29	338	11.7	3	61	26.0
Darius Hanks	10	26	328	12.6	1	36	32.8
Kenny Bell	13	17	255	15.0	2	41	19.6
Michael Williams	13	16	191	11.9	2	37	14.7
DeAndrew White	12	14	151	10.8	2	39	12.6
Brandon Gibson	13	14	140	10.0	1	23	10.8
Kevin Norwood	11	11	190	17.3	0	38	17.3
Eddie Lacy	12	11	131	11.9	0	48	10.9
Christion Jones	12	3	49	16.3	0	30	4.1
Blake Sims	5	2	18	9.0	0	10	3.6
Chris Underwood	13	2	12	6.0	0	8	0.9
Brian Vogler	9	1	6	6.0	0	6	0.7
Harrison Jones	8	1	5	5.0	0	5	0.6

DEFENSE

DEFENSE LEADERS

	GP	UA	A	TOTAL	TFL	SACK	INT	PBU
Dont'a Hightower	13	40	45	85	11.0	4.0	1	3
Mark Barron	13	43	25	68	5.0	1.0	2	5
Courtney Upshaw	13	36	15	51	17.0	8.5	1	0
Nico Johnson	13	25	22	47	6.5	1.0	1	3
DeQuan Menzie	13	27	14	41	4.0	1.5	1	11
Robert Lester	13	22	17	39	1.5	0	2	3
C.J. Mosley	11	17	20	37	4.5	2.0	1	2
Damion Square	13	13	19	32	7.0	1.0	0	1
Vinnie Sunseri	13	18	13	31	0	0	0	0
Dre Kirkpatrick	13	24	6	30	4.0	0	0	9
Jerrell Harris	13	17	12	29	3.5	0	0	0
DeMarcus Milliner	13	14	13	27	1.0	0	3	9
Trey Depriest	13	11	14	25	1.5	0	0	0

DEFENSE

DEFENSE LEADERS

	GP	UA	A	TOTAL	TFL	SACK	INT	PBU
Quinton Dial	12	10	14	24	3.0	1.0	0	0
Jesse Williams	13	10	14	24	4.0	0.5	0	1
Josh Chapman	12	10	13	23	3.5	1.0	0	2
Nick Gentry	12	11	12	23	6.0	4.5	0	0
Will Lowery	12	14	6	20	0.5	0	0	2
Ed Stinson	13	10	9	19	5.0	1.0	0	1
Alex Watkins	13	9	8	17	2.0	1.0	0	0
Ha'Seaon Clinton-Dix	13	5	6	11	0	0	0	2
Hardie Buck	13	3	6	9	0	0	0	0
Adrian Hubbard	9	3	6	9	1.5	0	0	0
Tana Patrick	10	2	5	7	0	0	0	0
Brandon Gibson	13	3	4	7	0	0	0	0
Cade Foster	13	4	2	6	0	0	0	0
Kelly Johnson	9	3	2	5	0	0	0	0
Jarrick Williams	7	4	1	5	0	0	0	0
Brandon Ivory	4	0	5	5	0	0	0	0
John Fulton	12	2	3	5	0	0	0	1
Undra Billingsley	13	1	3	4	1.0	0.5	0	0
Jeoffrey Pagan	6	0	4	4	0	0	0	0
Phelon Jones	9	2	2	4	0	0	1.0	0
Chris Jordan	6	0	3	3	0.5	0	0	0
Xzavier Dickson	7	2	1	3	1.5	0.5	0	0
DeAndrew White	12	2	0	2	0	0	0	0
Brad Smelley	13	1	1	2	0	0	0	0
Nick Perry	9	1	1	2	0	0	0	0
Ranzell Watkins	2	0	1	1	0	0	0	0
Carson Tinker	13	1	0	1	0	0	0	0
Christion Jones	12	1	0	1	0	0	0	0
D.J. Fluker	13	1	0	1	0	0	0	0
Jeremy Shelley	13	1	0	1	0	0	0	0
Michael Williams	13	1	0	1	0	0	0	0
Phillip Sims	8	1	0	1	0	0	0	0
Jalston Fowler	13	1	0	1	0	0	0	0
Eddie Lacy	12	0	1	1	0	0	0	0
AJ McCarron	13	1	0	1	0	0	0	0
Trent Richardson	13	1	0	1	0	0	0	0

INTERCEPTIONS

	NO.	YDS	AVG	TD	LG
DeMarcus Milliner	3	72	24.0	1	37
Robert Lester	2	30	15.0	0	30
Mark Barron	2	14	7.0	0	14
Phelon Jones	1	0	0.0	0	0
Dont'a Hightower	1	29	29.0	0	29
DeQuan Menzie	1	25	25.0	1	25
C.J. Mosley	1	1	1.0	0	1
Nico Johnson	1	2	2.0	0	2
Courtney Upshaw	1	45	45.0	1	45

FUMBLE RETURNS

	NO.	YDS	AVG	TD	LG
Nick Gentry	1	0	0.0	0	0
Dre Kirkpatrick	0	0	0.0	1	0

ALABAMA'S FINAL SEASON STATISTICS*

SPECIAL TEAMS

FIELD GOALS

	ATT	GOOD	LONG	BLOCKED
Jeremy Shelley	27	21	44	2
Cade Foster	9	2	46	0

PUNTING

	NO.	YDS	AVG	LG	BLOCKED
Cody Mandell	37	1434	38.8	50	0
Will Lowery	2	100	50.0	52	0

KICKOFFS

	NO.	YDS	AVG	TB	OB
Cade Foster	81	5128	63.3	5	1
Jeremy Shelley	9	496	55.1	0	0

PUNT RETURNS

	NO.	YDS	AVG	TD	LG
Marquis Maze	33	436	13.2	1	83
Christion Jones	3	33	11.0	0	18
DeAndrew White	2	34	17.0	0	20
Darius Hanks	1	4	4.0	0	4

KICK RETURNS

	NO.	YDS	AVG	TD	LG
Marquis Maze	12	342	28.5	0	70
Trent Richardson	3	66	22.0	0	24
Michael Williams	2	22	11.0	0	19
Darius Hanks	1	16	16.0	0	16
Chris Underwood	1	7	7.0	0	7
DeAndrew White	1	24	24.0	0	24
Christion Jones	1	32	32.0	0	32
DeMarcus Milliner	1	21	21.0	0	21

INDIVIDUAL GAME HIGHS

Rushes	32	Trent Richardson at Mississippi State (Nov 12, 2011)
		Trent Richardson vs Georgia Southern (Nov 19, 2011)
Yards Rushing	203	Trent Richardson at Auburn (Nov 26, 2011)
TD Rushes	4	Trent Richardson at Mississippi (Oct 15, 2011)
Long Rush	76	Trent Richardson at Mississippi (Oct 15, 2011)
Pass attempts	34	AJ McCarron vs LSU (Jan. 9, 2012)
Pass completions	23	AJ McCarron vs Vanderbilt (Oct 08, 2011)
		AJ McCarron vs LSU (Jan. 9, 2012)
Yards Passing	284	AJ McCarron vs Tennessee (Oct 22, 2011)
TD Passes	4	AJ McCarron vs Vanderbilt (Oct 08, 2011)
Long Pass	69	AJ McCarron vs Tennessee (Oct 22, 2011)
Receptions	9	Marquis Maze vs Vanderbilt (Oct 08, 2011)
Yards Receiving	118	Marquis Maze vs Kent State (Sep 03, 2011)
TD Receptions	2	DeAndrew White vs Vanderbilt (Oct 08, 2011)
		Brad Smelley vs Georgia Southern (Nov 19, 2011)
Long Reception	69	Marquis Maze vs Tennessee (Oct 22, 2011)
Field Goals	5	Jeremy Shelley vs LSU (Jan. 9, 2012)
Long Field Goal	46	Cade Foster vs LSU (Nov 05, 2011)
Punts	6	Cody Mandell at Penn State (Sep 10, 2011)
		Cody Mandell vs Arkansas (Sep 24, 2011)
Punting Avg	44.3	Cody Mandell vs LSU (Jan. 9, 2012)
Long Punt	52	Cody Mandell vs LSU (Jan. 9, 2012)
Punts inside 20	5	Cody Mandell at Florida (Oct 1, 2011)
Long Punt Return	83	Marquis Maze vs Arkansas (Sep 24, 2011)
Long Kickoff Return	70	Marquis Maze at Florida (Oct 1, 2011)
Tackles	11	Nico Johnson vs LSU (Nov 05, 2011)
		Mark Barron at Mississippi State (Nov 12, 2011)
		Dont'a Hightower at Mississippi State (Nov 12, 2011)
Sacks	2.0	Courtney Upshaw at Mississippi (Oct 15, 2011)
Tackles For Loss	3.0	Courtney Upshaw vs North Texas (Sep 17, 2011)
		Courtney Upshaw at Florida (Oct 1, 2011)
		Ed Stinson at Florida (Oct 1, 2011)
Interceptions	1	Phelon Jones vs Kent State (Sep 03, 2011)
		Mark Barron at Penn State (Sep 10, 2011)
		DeQuan Menzie vs Arkansas (Sep 24, 2011)
		DeMarcus Milliner vs Arkansas (Sep 24, 2011)
		Courtney Upshaw at Florida (Oct 1, 2011)
		DeMarcus Milliner vs Vanderbilt (Oct 08, 2011)
		Nico Johnson vs Vanderbilt (Oct 08, 2011)
		Robert Lester at Mississippi (Oct 15, 2011)
		Dont'a Hightower vs Tennessee (Oct 22, 2011)
		Mark Barron vs LSU (Nov 05, 2011)
		Robert Lester vs LSU (Nov 05, 2011)
		DeMarcus Milliner at Auburn (Nov 26, 2011)
		C.J. Mosley vs LSU (Jan. 9, 2012)

TEAM GAME HIGHS

Rushes	49	vs Georgia Southern (Nov 19, 2011)	First Downs	28	vs Georgia Southern (Nov 19, 2011)
Yards Rushing	389	at Mississippi (Oct 15, 2011)	Penalties	6	vs LSU (Nov 05, 2011)
Yards Per Rush	10.5	vs North Texas (Sep 17, 2011)			at Mississippi State (Nov 12, 2011)
TD Rushes	6	at Mississippi (Oct 15, 2011)			vs Georgia Southern (Nov 19, 2011)
Pass attempts	37	vs Kent State (Sep 03, 2011)	Penalty Yards	73	vs LSU (Nov 05, 2011)
Pass completions	26	vs Vanderbilt (Oct 08, 2011)	Turnovers	5	vs Kent State (Sep 03, 2011)
Yards Passing	299	vs Kent State (Sep 03, 2011)	Interceptions By	2	vs Arkansas (Sep 24, 2011)
Yards Per Pass	10.5	vs Tennessee (Oct 22, 2011)			vs Vanderbilt (Oct 08, 2011)
TD Passes	4	vs Vanderbilt (Oct 08, 2011)			vs LSU (Nov 05, 2011)
Total Plays	76	vs Vanderbilt (Oct 08, 2011)	Punts	6	at Penn State (Sep 10, 2011)
Total Offense	615	at Mississippi (Oct 15, 2011)			vs Arkansas (Sep 24, 2011)
Yards Per Play	9.5	vs North Texas (Sep 17, 2011)	Punting Avg	44.3	vs LSU (Jan. 9, 2012)
Points	52	at Mississippi (Oct 15, 2011)	Long Punt	52	vs LSU (Jan. 9, 2012)
Sacks By	5	at Mississippi (Oct 15, 2011)	Punts inside 20	5	at Florida (Oct 1, 2011)
		at Mississippi State (Nov 12, 2011)	Long Punt Return	83	vs Arkansas (Sep 24, 2011)

2011 ALABAMA ROSTER

NO	NAME	POS	HT/WT	YR	Hometown (Last School)
1	Dee Hart	RB	5-9/187	FR	Orlando, FL (Dr. Phillips)
2	Tana Patrick	LB	6-3/236	SO	Bridgeport, AL (North Jackson)
2	DeAndrew White	WR	6-0/181	FR	Houston, TX (North Shore)
3	Trent Richardson	RB	5-11/224	JR	Pensacola, FL (Escambia)
3	Vinnie Sunseri	S	6-0/217	FR	Tuscaloosa, AL (Northridge)
4	Mark Barron	S	6-2/218	SR	Mobile, AL (St. Paul's)
4	Marquis Maze	WR	5-10/180	SR	Birmingham, AL (Tarrant HS)
5	Ronald Carswell	WR	6-0/180	FR	Macon, GA (Westside)
5	Jerrell Harris	LB	6-3/242	SR	Gadsden, AL (Gadsden City)
6	Blake Sims	ATH	6-0/212	FR	Gainesville, GA (Gainesville)
6	Ha'Seaon Clinton-Dix	DB	6-1/203	FR	Orlando, FL (Dr. Phillips)
7	Kenny Bell	WR	6-1/175	SO	Rayville, LA (Rayville)
8	Duron Carter	WR	6-4/210	JR	Coffeyville, KS (Coffeyville CC)
8	Jeoffrey Pagan	DE	6-4/272	FR	Asheville, NC (Asheville)
9	Phelon Jones	DB	5-11/194	SR	Mobile, AL (McGill-Toolen)
9	Nick Williams	WR	5-10/185	SO	Ft. Lauderdale, FL (St. Thomas Aquinas)
10	John Fulton	CB	6-0/187	SO	Manning, SC (Manning)
10	AJ McCarron	QB	6-4/205	SO	Mobile, AL (St. Paul's)
11	Ranzell Watkins	DB	5-9/170	SO	Charlotte, NC (Independence)
11	Brandon Gibson	WR	6-2/194	SR	Mobile, AL (UMS-Wright)
12	Phillip Ely	QB	6-1/187	FR	Tampa, FL (Plant)
13	Diege Barry	DB	5-10/180	JR	Mobile, AL (St. Paul's)
14	Phillip Sims	QB	6-2/217	FR	Chesapeake, VA (Oscar Smith)
15	Darius Hanks	WR	6-0/185	SR	Norcross, GA (Norcross)
16	Bradley Sylve	WR	5-11/170	FR	Port Sulpher, La. (South Plaquemines)
17	Brad Smelley	TE	6-3/229	SR	Tuscaloosa, AL (American Christian)
18	Levi Cook	DB	5-10/190	JR	Decatur, AL (Decatur)
18	Morgan Ogilvie	QB	6-0/198	FR	Mountain Brook, AL (Mountain Brook)
19	Jonathan Atchison	LB	6-2/240	SO	Atlanta, GA (Douglass)
19	Ronald James	WR	5-8/166	JR	Castro Valley, CA (Bishop O'Dowd)
20	Nate Carlson	TE	6-4/236	JR	Birmingham, AL (Air Force)
20	Jarrick Williams	DB	6-1/210	SO	Mobile, AL (Blount)
21	Brent Calloway	RB	6-1/217	FR	Russellville, AL (Russellville)
21	Dre Kirkpatrick	DB	6-3/192	JR	Gadsden, AL (Gadsden City)
22	Christion Jones	WR	5-11/175	FR	Adamsville, AL (Minor)
24	Nathan McAlister	WR	5-11/165	FR	Russellville, AL (Russellville)
24	DeQuan Menzie	CB	6-0/198	SR	Columbus, GA (Copia-Lincoln CC)
25	Caleb Castille	DB	5-11/170	FR	Birmingham, AL (Briarwood Christian)
25	Danny Woodson, Jr.	WR	6-1/205	FR	Mobile, Ala. (LeFlore)
25	Ben Howell	RB	5-9/202	JR	Gordo, AL (Gordo)
26	Nick Tinker	RB	5-10/207	SO	Ralph, AL (Tuscaloosa County)
26	Jabriel Washington	DB	5-11/165	FR	Jackson, TN (Trinity Christian)
27	Nick Perry	DB	6-1/205	SO	Prattville, AL (Prattville)
28	Dee Milliner	CB	6-1/196	SO	Millbrook, AL (Stanhope Elmore)
29	Will Lowery	DB	5-9/180	JR	Hoover, AL (Hoover)
29	Cody Mandell	P	6-4/202	SO	Lafayette, LA (Acadiana)
30	Dont'a Hightower	LB	6-4/260	JR	Lewisburg, TN (Marshall County)
31	Kelly Johnson	SN	6-3/230	SR	Bluffton, SC (Providence Day)
31	Jerrod Bierbower	DB	6-1/180	FR	Dublin, OH (Coffman)
31	John Baites	TE	6-4/231	SR	Hendersonville, TN (Beech)
32	C.J. Mosley	LB	6-2/234	SO	Theodore, AL (Theodore)
33	Trey DePriest	LB	6-2/242	FR	Springfield, OH (Springfield)
34	Hunter Bush	DB	5-11/195	JR	Wetumpka, AL (Wetumpka)
35	Nico Johnson	LB	6-3/245	JR	Andalusia, AL (Andalusia)
36	Chris Jordan	LB	6-3/240	SR	Brentwood, TN (Brentwood Academy)
37	Robert Lester	S	6-2/210	JR	Foley, AL (Foley)
40	DeMarcus DuBose	LB	6-1/240	SR	Montgomery, AL (Jefferson Davis)
41	Courtney Upshaw	LB	6-2/265	SR	Eufaula, AL (Eufaula)
42	Adrian Hubbard	LB	6-6/237	FR	Lawrenceville, GA (Norcross)
42	Eddie Lacy	RB	6-0/220	SO	Geismar, LA (Dutchtown)
43	Cade Foster	K	6-1/216	SO	Southlake, TX (Southlake Carroll)
43	Taylor Conant	WR	6-0/195	JR	Tuscaloosa, AL (Tuscaloosa Academy)
43	Sam Kearns	DB	5-6/155	SR	Mobile, AL (McGill-Toolen)
44	LaMichael Fanning	DL	6-7/275	FR	Hamilton, GA (Harris County)
44	Jay Williams	P	6-3/221	FR	Thomasville, AL (Thomasville)
45	Jalston Fowler	FB	6-1/246	SO	Mobile, AL (Vigor)
46	William Strickland	WR	6-0/191	SR	Tuscaloosa, AL (Northridge)
47	Xzavier Dickson	LB/DL	6-3/240	FR	Griffin, GA (Griffin)
48	Tommy Keys	FB	6-2/230	FR	West Point, MS (West Point)
48	Rowdy Harrell	LB	6-0/219	SR	Moundville, AL (Hale County)
49	Ed Stinson	DE	6-4/279	SO	Homestead, FL (South Dade)
49	M.K. Taylor	SN	5-10/208	SO	Anniston, AL (Oxford)
50	Robert Cramer	SN	6-0/240	FR	Hoover, AL (Hoover)
51	Wilson Love	DL	6-3/276	FR	Mountain Brook, AL (Mountain Brook)
51	Carson Tinker	LS	6-1/220	JR	Murfreesboro, TN (Riverdale)
52	Alfred McCullough	OL	6-2/311	SR	Athens, AL (Athens)
53	Anthony Orr	DL	6-4/258	FR	Madison, AL (Sparkman)
54	Jesse Williams	DL	6-4/319	JR	Brisbane, Australia, (Western Arizona CC)
54	Russell Raines	OL	6-2/281	SO	Satsuma, AL (Satsuma)
55	Josh Dickerson	LB	6-1/235	SO	Evans, GA (Lakeside)
56	William Ming	DL	6-3/283	SO	Athens, AL (Athens)
57	Aaron Joiner	OL	6-2/275	JR	Florence, AL (Florence)
57	D.J. Pettway	DE	6-2/272	FR	Pensacola, FL (Pensacola Catholic)
58	Nick Gentry	DL	6-1/284	SR	Prattville, AL (Prattville)
59	Arie Kouandijo	OT	6-5/335	FR	Beltsville, MD (DeMatha Catholic)
61	Anthony Steen	G	6-3/303	SO	Lambert, MS (Lee Academy)
62	Brandon Ivory	NT	6-4/308	FR	Memphis, TN (East)
63	Kellen Williams	OL	6-3/305	SO	Lawrenceville, GA (Brookwood)
65	Chance Warmack	G	6-3/320	JR	Atlanta, GA (Westlake)
67	John Michael Boswell	OL	6-5/300	SR	Northport, AL (Tuscaloosa County)
68	Isaac Luatua	OL	6-2/299	FR	La Mirada, CA (La Mirada)
68	Austin Gray	OL	6-0/309	SO	Woodstock, GA (Alan C. Pope)
69	David Blalock	OL	6-5/261	SR	Charlotte, NC (Providence)
70	Ryan Kelly	OL	6-5/281	FR	West Chester OH (Lakota West)
71	Cyrus Kouandijo	OL	6-6/322	FR	Hyattsville, MD (DeMatha Catholic)
72	Tyler Love	T	6-6/307	Jr.	Mountain Brook, AL (Mountain Brook)
73	William Vlachos	C	6-1/294	SR	Birmingham, AL (Mountain Brook)
74	Allen Skelton	OL	6-1/267	JR	Coker, AL (Tuscaloosa County)
75	Barrett Jones	G	6-5/311	JR	Memphis, TN (Evangelical Christian)
76	D.J. Fluker	OL	6-6/335	SO	Foley, AL (Foley)
78	Chad Lindsay	OL	6-2/287	FR	The Woodlands, TX (The Woodlands)
79	Austin Shepherd	OT	6-5/321	FR	Buford, GA (North Gwinnett)
80	Marvin Shinn	WR	6-3/193	FR	Prichard, AL (Vigor)
81	Hardie Buck	WR	5-9/190	JR	Birmingham, AL (Vestavia Hills)
82	Harrison Jones	TE	6-4/248	FR	Memphis, TN (Evangelical Christian)
83	Kevin Norwood	WR	6-2/193	SO	D'Iberville, MS (D'Iberville)
84	Brian Vogler	TE	6-7/252	FR	Columbus, GA (Brookstone)
85	Malcolm Faciane	TE	6-5/259	FR	Picayune, MS (Picayune Memorial)
86	Undra Billingsley	DE	6-2/288	JR	Birmingham, AL (Woodlawn)
87	Chris Underwood	TE	6-4/243	SR	Vestavia Hills, AL (Vestavia Hills)
88	Michael Bowman	WR	6-4/225	SO	Rossville, GA (Ridgeland)
89	Michael Williams	TE	6-6/269	JR	Reform, AL (Pickens County)
90	Quinton Dial	DL	6-6/294	JR	Pinson, AL (East Mississippi CC)
90	Jeremy Shelley	K	5-10/165	JR	Raleigh, NC (Broughton)
91	Alex Watkins	LB	6-3/234	SR	Brownsville, TN (Haywood)
92	Damion Square	DE	6-3/285	JR	Houston, TX (Yates)
93	Chris Bonds	DE	6-4/269	SO	Columbia, SC (Richland Northeast)
95	Brandon Lewis	TE	6-3/288	JR	Pleasant Grove, AL (East Mississippi CC)
99	Josh Chapman	NT	6-1/310	SR	Hoover, AL (Hoover)